THE COMPLETE DAIRY-FREE COOKBOOK

➤ LEMON CURD, PAGE 160

The Complete Dairy-Free Cookbook

125+ Delicious, Family-Friendly Recipes

PAMELA ELLGEN

ROCKRIDGE
PRESS

Interior and Cover Designer: Karmen Lizzul
Art Producer: Janice Ackerman
Associate Editor: Maxine Marshall
Production Manager: Jose Olivera
Production Editor: Melissa Edeburn

Cover Photography by Andrew Purcell. Food styling by Carrie Purcell (title page).

Interior Photography: ii: ©The Picture Pantry/StockFood; vi: ©Jennifer Davick; p. 2: © Coco Lang/Gräfe & Unzer Verlag/StockFood; p. 11: ©Hélène Dujardin; p. 12: ©Trent Lanz/Stocksy; p. 20: ©Brigitte Sporrer/StockFood; p. 30: ©Lisa Rees/StockFood; p. 39: ©Evi Abeler; p. 48: ©Magdalena Hendey/StockFood; p. 54: ©Tara Donne; p. 62: ©Mathias Neubauer/Gräfe & Unzer Verlag /StockFood; p. 70: ©Darren Muir; p. 76: ©Darren Muir; p. 82: ©Jonathan Gregson/StockFood; p. 92: ©Amy Johnson; p. 98: ©Jonathan Gregson/StockFood; p. 108: ©Darren Muir; p. 116: ©Michael Wissing/StockFood; p. 124: ©Laura Flippen; p. 132: ©Eising Studio - Food Photo & Video/StockFood; p. 146: ©Darren Muir; p. 150: ©Nadine Greeff; p. 154: ©Darren Muir; p. 163: ©Emulsion Studio; p. 168: ©Mari Moilanen/StockFood; p. 175: ©Nat and Cody Gantz; p. 182: ©Marti Sans/Stocksy (copyright page)

Paperback ISBN: 978-1-63807-974-3 | eBook ISBN: 978-1-63807-560-8
R0

CONTENTS

INTRODUCTION

One of my earliest memories is of speeding down the interstate in the front seat of my dad's Ford Thunderbird on the way to the hospital, hours after my bedtime. I tried to breathe, but every breath brought on wheezing and coughing that racked my seven-year-old body.

I was having an asthma attack triggered by dairy. I had several more attacks during my childhood and adolescence. I carried an inhaler and knew, especially after a cold, that I was particularly susceptible to them. Even the thought of macaroni and cheese could leave me breathless.

As I grew older, I wanted to believe I had outgrown the allergy. And, in some ways, I had. My asthma attacks were mostly a thing of the past. So, I indulged in pizza, ice cream, and plenty of artisan cheeses.

However, like so many adults, I eventually began to suspect that dairy might be the trouble behind numerous seemingly unrelated health concerns—gastrointestinal distress, mood changes, acne, and seasonal allergies. Whether these symptoms represented a true dairy allergy no longer mattered. When I cut dairy from my diet for good, these issues resolved themselves. The change was remarkable, and my newfound health made the sacrifice worth it.

It's been a challenge, but I've found recipes that satisfy my cravings for nearly all my favorite foods. Some things can never be replaced—triple-cream Brie, for example. But my palate quickly changed to appreciate a dairy-free lifestyle—I even prefer to drink my coffee black now! And I've learned a lot along the way.

In this book, there's something for everyone. The easiest dairy-free route is simply to pick up store-bought analogs of dairy products—dairy-free cream cheese, dairy-free cheese shreds, and so on. And in some instances, I do use those substitutes. But I prefer to diversify the ingredients I use, including white beans, nuts, and other naturally dairy-free ingredients, to create creamy textures and divine flavors.

I'm excited to help bring new choices to your plate, and I hope these recipes help you feel great as you enjoy a dairy-free lifestyle that's satisfying, fun, and delicious!

PART ONE

How to Be Dairy-Free

CHAPTER ONE

Understanding the Dairy-Free Diet

When you first embark on a dairy-free diet, you might feel as though dairy is in everything. Dairy products fill the pages of most cookbooks and sneak their way into ingredient lists of seemingly innocuous foods. The good news is, armed with a little knowledge and the recipes in this cookbook, you can navigate the supermarket safely and smartly and create delicious meals you and your family will crave. This chapter gives you the basics to get started right away.

What Is a Dairy-Free Diet?

Dairy products contain milk made from mammals—including cows, sheep, and goats—or from the by-products of milk production. Common dairy products include butter, cheese, cream, ice cream, milk, and yogurt. For the newly diagnosed with a dairy allergy, intolerance, or sensitivity, knowing that eggs are not a dairy food may come as a relief.

Some people restrict dairy from their diet for health reasons, such as a milk allergy or lactose intolerance. Others avoid dairy for environmental or ethical concerns or religious reasons. Whatever your reason for giving up dairy, doing so can have a profound and positive impact on your health.

A strict dairy-free diet is essential for vegans or people with life-threatening allergies, which means the obvious sources of dairy should be avoided, as well as all foods that contain a by-product of dairy, such as caseinates, whey proteins, and hydrolysates (see Other Names for Dairy, page 6). Others choose to follow a generally dairy-free diet and avoid consuming obvious sources of dairy, but don't necessarily worry about foods that may contain a dairy by-product. This book follows a strict dairy-free diet.

Dairy-Free for Better Health

You may be dealing with a new health diagnosis that requires you to adopt a dairy-free diet, or perhaps you suspect that dairy may be the culprit behind chronic health issues. Let's look, in some detail, at the top health reasons to cut dairy from your diet.

MILK ALLERGY

Milk allergy is an immune reaction to milk that can involve hives, swelling, vomiting, wheezing, and potentially even anaphylaxis or death. A diagnosis is made by employing a food elimination diet, measuring antibodies in the blood, administering a skin-prick test, or some combination of these methods. The only proven treatment for a milk allergy is strict dairy avoidance. However, oral immunotherapy, which involves consuming minuscule but ever-increasing amounts of the allergen, has shown some promise in clinical settings.

A true milk allergy is relatively rare in adults, affecting only about 4 percent of the adult population. Conversely, milk allergy is the most common allergy among children. Additionally, because milk proteins can pass through breast milk to a breastfed baby, nursing mothers of children who are allergic to milk should also avoid consuming dairy products. Fortunately, the vast majority of children outgrow their milk allergy by the age of five.

LACTOSE INTOLERANCE

Lactose intolerance is the inability to digest lactose, a sugar found in milk, because of an absence of the digestive enzyme lactase in the body. This condition involves symptoms such as bloating, diarrhea, gas, and nausea, which occur when undigested lactose passes into the colon and feeds bacteria there. Lactose intolerance affects far more people than milk allergy does, perhaps as much as 65 percent of the global population. Individuals in Asia and central Africa are especially likely to be lactose intolerant, with one explanation for this intolerance being that before the advent of agriculture, human beings did not consume milk after weaning in early childhood, and their production of lactase ended. Lactase persistence, the body's manufacture of the lactase enzyme into adulthood, only began developing in European populations relatively recently, around 2000 BCE, and even more recently in cultures that did not rely on animal milk for food past weaning.

FOOD SENSITIVITY

Beyond lactose intolerance and true food allergies, which involve an immediate immune response, food sensitivities can cause reactions in people who are sensitive to dairy proteins.

These reactions may include digestive problems, mood disturbances, skin changes, or other physical symptoms.

The best way to determine if you have a food sensitivity is to remove the suspected food from your diet for a period of 30 days, or until your symptoms subside, then reintroduce the food to see if a reaction occurs.

One explanation for food sensitivities is the "leaky gut" theory, which asserts that environmental and dietary factors have damaged the lining of the gut, creating spaces between the cells that line the intestinal tract. Larger protein molecules migrate from the digestive tract into the bloodstream, where the immune system mounts a response to these perceived invaders. This response may manifest as physical symptoms and potentially contribute to autoimmune disorders.

PLANT-BASED DIET

A plant-based diet eliminates all animal products, including dairy, eggs, fish, meat, and poultry, and instead seeks all nutrition from plant sources. Numerous studies illustrate the health benefits of a plant-based diet, including reduced risks for heart disease, high blood pressure, obesity, type 2 diabetes, and other metabolic disorders, and improved gut microbiome diversity (a fascinating subject in itself), reduced cancer risk, and greater longevity.

And although a plant-based diet and a vegan diet may look identical in practice, they differ in that vegans avoid animal products in their lifestyle as well as in their diet and do so for ethical reasons, not solely for dietary reasons.

DAIRY SENSITIVITY CONNECTIONS

Individuals who have a dairy allergy are also more likely to be allergic to one of the other top eight allergens. In addition to dairy, these allergens are eggs, fish, wheat, peanuts, shellfish, soy, and tree nuts. US law requires these allergens to be listed on food labels. Unfortunately, proteins found in goat's milk are similar to those in cow's milk and may also cause an allergic reaction. Interestingly, as many as 20 percent of children who are allergic to milk are also allergic to beef!

The recipes in this book are designed with these sensitivities in mind, and feature the "Allergen-Free" label for dishes that are free from all of the top eight allergens, or "Make Allergen-Free" for dishes that contain ingredients that can be easily swapped to make them allergen-free.

Reading Food Labels

Whatever your reasons for adopting a dairy-free diet, you'll want to know which foods contain dairy and which foods are at a high risk for cross-contamination with dairy. This section will help you decipher sometimes-tricky food labels and screen for ingredients that contain dairy.

Be especially wary of foods labeled "nondairy," a term used often on whipped cream, coffee creamer, and other processed foods that legally can contain derivatives of dairy. (How's that for confusing?) Instead, seek out the label "dairy-free."

DAIRY FOODS

Here are the more obvious sources of dairy you probably already know to avoid.

→ Butter
→ Buttermilk
→ Cheese
→ Cottage cheese
→ Cream
→ Custard
→ Ghee
→ Half-and-half
→ Milk
→ Pudding
→ Sour cream
→ Yogurt

MAY CONTAIN DAIRY

These foods may contain dairy, but not always. Read the food label or ask the person who prepared it whether dairy is present.

→ Artificial butter flavor
→ Baked goods
→ Caramel candies
→ Chocolate
→ Lunch meat, hot dogs, sausages
→ Margarine
→ Nondairy products
→ Nougat
→ White/Alfredo sauce

OTHER NAMES FOR DAIRY

Be on the lookout for these words that indicate the presence of dairy.

→ Casein (a protein in milk)
→ Casein hydrolysate
→ Caseinates
→ Diacetyl
→ Lactalbumin
→ Lactalbumin phosphate
→ Lactoferrin
→ Lactose (the main sugar in milk)
→ Lactulose
→ Milk protein hydrolysate
→ Recaldent
→ Rennet casein
→ Sour milk solids
→ Tagatose
→ Whey (the watery part of milk)
→ Whey protein hydrolysate

Getting Calcium and Vitamin D

The first thing people—even random strangers—ask when they hear that you don't eat dairy is, "But how do you get your calcium?" The dairy industry has made it seem like an unquestionable fact that cow's milk is the ideal source of calcium for humans.

However, a panel of scientists at the United States Department of Agriculture (USDA) came to a different conclusion in 2001 when they investigated the claims made in those ubiquitous "milk mustache" ads. They found that there was no evidence that dairy consumption alone builds strong bones or prevents osteoporosis. The panel also found that whole milk consumption may contribute to heart disease and prostate cancer.

HOW MUCH DO YOU NEED?

Undeniably, calcium and vitamin D are essential nutrients for human health. The Recommended Daily Allowance (RDA) for calcium is 1,000 milligrams for men and women ages 19 to 50, increasing to 1,200 milligrams a day for women over 50 (for men, it remains 1,000). The RDA for vitamin D is 600 IU (15 mcg) for men and women ages 19 to 70.

Calcium and vitamin D work in tandem—among other benefits, vitamin D increases calcium absorption in the gut and maintains calcium and phosphate balance in the body to ensure normal bone mineralization.

VITAMIN D AND CALCIUM SOURCES

Rest assured, you will get your calcium on a dairy-free diet. Calcium is available from a wide array of foods unrelated to dairy. In fact, some of these foods have additional health-promoting elements, including antioxidants, fiber, minerals, and vitamins. Foods that naturally contain calcium include almonds, beans, bok choy, broccoli, collard and turnip greens, edamame, figs, kale, oranges, salmon, sardines, tofu, and watercress. Some processed foods, such as orange juice, soy milk, and even chocolate, are also fortified with calcium.

Few foods in nature contain vitamin D, according to the National Institutes of Health, and the only reason milk is seen as a good source of this vitamin is because it has been fortified with it. Other foods are also fortified with vitamin D, including breakfast cereals, orange juice, and other processed foods. Whole food options offering vitamin D include beef liver, egg yolks, salmon, swordfish, and tuna.

The primary method by which our bodies obtain adequate (80 to 90 percent) amounts of vitamin D is exposure to the sun via bare skin (sunscreen blocks the rays that help your body manufacture this vitamin). The amount of time required for your skin to produce adequate vitamin D varies based on the time of year, location, your skin color, and how much skin you have exposed (more is better). It's essential to note that adequate vitamin D production can occur in half the time it takes for your skin to begin to burn when exposed to the sun.

Beyond getting adequate sunlight, other commonsense lifestyle factors can improve your vitamin and mineral stockpile, such as ceasing smoking, exercising regularly, and limiting caffeinated beverages and sodas.

SUPPLEMENTS

Nutrition supplements may be helpful to ensure adequate levels of calcium and vitamin D, especially on a dairy-free diet. However, it's important to consult with your physician to have your nutritional status tested before you start taking pills.

Calcium supplements come in the form of calcium citrate, malate, and carbonate, with carbonate being the most common (it's the primary ingredient in Tums, for example). However, carbonate is the least absorbable form of calcium and should be taken with food to be most effective. Some supplements offer a combination of calcium types. Supplements are best divided into multiple doses, because the body cannot absorb large amounts of calcium at one time.

Vitamin D supplements are an option for people living in extreme latitudes, those with darker skin, and older individuals. However, supplementation is a tricky thing, as it can result in arterial calcification, kidney stones, and high concentrations of calcium in the blood—good reasons to talk with your doctor before taking any supplements.

Dairy-Free Living Success

After living strictly dairy-free for the past four years, I know the ins and outs of staying dairy-free, and I know I'm supposed to tell you it's always been easy. But, at least initially, living dairy-free can be challenging. You might be saying goodbye to some of your favorite foods, which are often tied to deeply personal experiences and cultural traditions. You may also be dealing with children who aren't thrilled that you're taking away their beloved dishes (and if so, I want to reassure you that there is a mac 'n' cheese recipe in this book!).

You may be asking, "What in the world *should* I eat?" Here are my tips and tricks for going dairy-free with grace.

HANDLING CRAVINGS

There are a few strategies that work for me when it comes to handling cravings. First, I go without. Yes, you read that right, but keep reading; I'll get to a solution. Most dairy-free substitutes on the market don't cut it for me. There are some substitutes that are acceptable, but most just remind me of what I'm missing, and they aren't all that healthy anyway. Instead of accepting an unsatisfactory substitute, I skip the cream in my coffee and mostly choose family grill night over pizza night.

Second, I invest a little more energy into preparing delicious foods that are naturally dairy-free. You'll definitely want to try my Coconut-Ginger Pork Tenderloin Skewers (page 103). In fact, most Asian-inspired cuisine is naturally dairy-free and tastes amazing. When you look beyond the standard American diet, a world of naturally dairy-free cuisine awaits. By exploring the options, you're likely to develop a whole list of new foods to crave— and enjoy!

Finally, going back to my first strategy, I do sometimes splurge on dairy-free prepared foods when a craving for something creamy, salty, or sweet strikes. There are some good options: Earth Balance Buttery Spread, Miyoko's Creamery products, Tofutti Better Than Sour Cream, and Trader Joe's Soy Creamy Cherry Chocolate Chip ice cream are some of my favorites. I also developed recipes for this book that offer some of the features of dairy that I missed most—its saltiness and creaminess especially. I think my Miso-Tahini Ice Cream (page 159) is to die for, and Plant-Based Parmesan (page 27) is close enough to the real thing that it does the trick.

For some people, dairy cravings go beyond simply missing your favorite foods. In the book *The Cheese Trap*, Dr. Neal Barnard argues that dairy contains mild opiates that attach to the same brain receptors that heroin and morphine do, causing us to eat more than we should and keep coming back for more. Fortunately, when dairy is removed from the diet, the cravings eventually subside. For some people, this change happens within a few days. For others, it can take as long as two weeks for cravings to cease.

DINING OUT

Some decisions are easy: you know to pass on the cheesy pizza and loaded nachos when dining out, but it's also important to be aware of hidden sources of dairy found in restaurant cooking. Things you would never think contain dairy, such as roasted vegetables or pan-seared meats, are often topped with butter just before serving. Many baked goods contain dairy, as do mashed potatoes, pancakes, scrambled eggs, and other seemingly non-dairy foods.

I recommend calling restaurants ahead or checking their websites to learn about their dairy-free options. Vegan restaurants are an easy solution, but not if you're looking for meat. Restaurants serving Chinese, Japanese, and Thai cuisines are usually completely dairy-free. When you arrive, inform your server of your needs, ask them to recommend some dairy-free options on the menu, and request that the chef please skip the butter on your dish.

EATING AT SOCIAL GATHERINGS

Dietary restrictions have become more commonplace, lessening the feeling of social stigma and making it easier to navigate social gatherings. It's good practice to inform your host of your dietary restrictions when you accept an invitation. I usually offer to bring a side or main dish to share. If it's a small gathering, such as dinner at someone's house, I often suggest the many things I still do eat. Most hosts find this helpful, because they may have never considered what foods do or don't contain dairy (and, in my case, gluten). If I suspect the situation may not provide sufficient dairy-free options, I'll eat a small protein-rich snack before the gathering.

KIDS' PARTIES AND SCHOOL CELEBRATIONS

Birthday parties can be so hard for little ones who sit there watching their friends devour cupcakes, ice cream, and pizza. I don't want my children to feel deprived or socially awkward, so on these occasions, I tell the host about their dietary restrictions and offer to bring something they can eat. I try to match my food as closely as possible to whatever else is being served. For birthday parties in the classroom, it's easiest for me to supply the teacher with a cache of individually wrapped treats that my kids can have whenever birthday parties pop up throughout the year. I also have tried keeping a stash of cupcakes in my freezer for such occasions. I can easily defrost them one at a time and send them to school when I know another kid is celebrating a birthday.

CHAPTER TWO

The Joy of Dairy-Free Cooking

Dairy-free cooking has become more than a necessity in my kitchen—it has become fun! I love finding alternatives to dairy that taste delicious and keep my whole family healthy. There's something particularly satisfying about creating a new ice cream recipe or discovering a fabulous hot nacho cheese dip. Soon you, too, will be having fun (yes, fun) cooking without dairy.

Preparing Your Kitchen

Naturally, a well-stocked pantry and a refrigerator filled with dairy-free foods for meals and snacks make cooking easy. Grocery shopping is actually more enjoyable than you might imagine. After I changed my diet, I gave myself permission to spend a little more money than usual to try new foods I might have otherwise considered a splurge.

Preparing the kitchen also involves removing any items containing dairy, both the obvious sources and those hiding behind the sneaky names listed in chapter 1 (see page 6). Some couples and families in which only one person needs to be dairy-free might choose to leave dairy foods in the house. Others choose to go completely dairy-free. In my home, we usually opt for the latter. It's just not fair for one kid to get a loaded pizza and the other to get a dairy-free version while sitting at the same table. (We have tried several brands of dairy-free cheese, and my son Brad can always tell the difference.)

Essential Equipment

Beyond the basics—cutting boards, knives, pans, pots, and other utensils—a few kitchen appliances and gadgets will make dairy-free cooking easier, tastier, and more fun. Fortunately, there are only a few items that I consider essential to cooking a dairy-free diet. These items are used primarily to make staples, such as almond milk, which saves money, eliminates packaging waste, and avoids the thickeners and preservatives in store-bought varieties.

Blender: for making smoothies, plant-based milks, and sauces

Food processor: for chopping and grating vegetables, and grinding nuts

Ice cream maker: for preparing homemade dairy-free ice cream

Nut milk bag: a reusable muslin or nylon bag with a drawstring for straining plant-based milks and cheeses

MAKE YOUR OWN NUT MILK BAG

As the saying goes, necessity is the mother of invention, so if you find yourself without a nut milk bag, make your own. Spread a few layers of cheesecloth over a large metal strainer and pour the nut milk mixture through it. Gather the corners of the cheesecloth and twist to squeeze out as much liquid as you can.

Stocking a Dairy-Free Pantry

Here are the most important basic ingredients to have on hand for easy preparation of dairy-free meals, snacks, and drinks.

Almonds: for making almond milk

Cashews: for making cashew cream and sauces

Coconut milk: for making curries and soups, and using in place of cream when the flavor is complementary. Alternatively, homemade Coconut Milk (page 25) can be made from shredded unsweetened coconut.

Dairy-free butter: to replace butter as a condiment and in cooking (but generally not in baking). I recommend Earth Balance Buttery Spread. If you have a soy allergy, make sure to purchase the soy-free version and use it when making recipes labeled "Make Allergen-Free" that call for this ingredient.

Dairy-free chocolate chips: for making cookies, trail mix, and other sweet treats

Dairy-free sour cream: for making sauces, thickening soups, and as a condiment

Nonhydrogenated vegetable shortening: for baking

Nutritional yeast: for giving sauces and dips a cheesy flavor. Available online and at health foods stores in bulk or prepackaged. (This is not a leavener like the yeast used for baking or brewing.)

Silken tofu: for thickening sauces and making desserts (different from soft or firm tofu)

How to Cook without Dairy

You can approach dairy-free cooking in a few ways. The first and easiest way is to choose naturally dairy-free recipes. This eliminates the frustration of trying to replicate a traditional dairy-filled recipe and being disappointed with the results. Beef Bourguignon, for example, is usually naturally dairy-free, so it tastes just like it should. But, eventually, this approach can get boring, especially if you miss your favorites that traditionally include dairy.

The second option is to make one-to-one swaps with prepared foods, such as by using dairy-free butter, cream cheese, or sour cream for the dairy version. This approach is convenient, and many store-bought dairy-free foods are delicious and taste close to the dairy versions. However, some versions miss the mark, are otherwise void of nutrition, or may contain other ingredients you want to avoid.

Finally, you can make your own swaps using a variety of ingredients and combinations designed to mimic the taste and texture of dairy foods. This requires a lot of experimentation, or you can let someone else do the testing and follow their recipe.

I'll do anything that's required to result in a satisfying dish, so in this book I use all three approaches to cooking dairy-free. I provide many recipes that never had dairy to begin with. I use store-bought replacements for dairy in a few recipes. And I offer many recipes that use novel ingredients to stand in for dairy.

COMMON SUBSTITUTIONS

Butter: When cooking, I use canola oil instead of butter. The oil has a higher smoke point, so it doesn't burn at higher temperatures, and it has a neutral flavor. I also opt for olive oil or coconut oil if the flavor is desirable in the recipe. In baking, I use nonhydrogenated vegetable shortening or coconut oil in place of butter. However, because butter isn't pure fat and contains some liquid, I add about 1 tablespoon of plant-based milk or water for every 1 cup butter called for in the recipe.

Cheese sauce: I have found several substitutions that work as a cheesy sauce alternative, including blended cashews, silken tofu, and white sauce made with oil, starch, and plant-based milk. White beans and other vegetables can also be blended into a convincing sauce. Check out my Mac 'n' Cheese (page 136) and Creamy Artichoke and Pesto Pizza (page 135) for two different cheese sauce options, in addition to the cheesy sauce recipes in chapters 6 and 12 (see Nacho Cheese Dip, page 73, and Cheese Sauce, Two Ways, page 181).

Cream: Full-fat coconut milk and Cashew Cream (page 23) work well as substitutes for dairy-based cream in cooking and baking. When chilled, store-bought coconut milk can be whipped into soft, fluffy peaks just like whipped cream.

Hard cheeses: I love my Plant-Based Parmesan (page 27), which combines cashews, garlic powder, salt, and nutritional yeast in a crumbly, dairy-free triumph. It is not built for slicing but is delicious sprinkled over pasta, pizza, salad—okay, pretty much everything!

Milk: Plant-based milks work well in most recipes calling for milk. I use my basic Plain or Vanilla Nut Milk (page 22) in most recipes calling for milk, and it fills the need. You can also use Soy Milk (page 24). Rice Milk (page 26), however, has a thinner texture and should be used only when that consistency is desirable.

Soft cheeses: For fresh soft cheeses such as chèvre, queso fresco, and ricotta, I usually opt for a nut-based cheese. I like the flavors of blanched almonds, cashews, and macadamia nuts best, and I add some lemon juice or vinegar for acidity. Firm tofu can also be pulsed in a food processor to give it the consistency of ricotta.

Yogurt: For cooking and baking, coconut milk with a splash of lemon juice stands in nicely for yogurt in many recipes. Store-bought dairy-free yogurts are hit or miss, with many containing nothing more than plant-based milk, thickener, probiotics, and loads of sugar. You can also make your own dairy-free yogurt, but it is more difficult to get good results than when making homemade yogurt with dairy.

Plant-Based Milks

Plant-based milks are healthy substitutes for dairy milk, and they taste pretty good, too. Each variety of nondairy milk has a slightly different flavor, and the milks themselves often vary greatly with regard to their nutritional profiles. What the nondairy milks don't have are antibiotics, cholesterol, hormones, or lactose.

You can purchase all of the plant-based milks listed here at the grocery store, or make your own at home. This book offers a full chapter of such recipes. I like the convenience of purchasing plant-based milk, but I prefer to avoid the emulsifiers, stabilizers, thickeners, and other additives that often reside in store-bought milks. Plus, I think the milks I make at home taste better! The one exception is that when cooking, I prefer store-bought canned coconut milk and coconut cream.

The table below offers nutrition facts for 1-cup servings of the most common plant-based milks. Note the two entries for coconut milk. The first entry is a coconut milk beverage, usually stored in the refrigerated section of the grocery store or found in shelf-stable cartons. The second is for canned coconut milk used in cooking but not as a beverage by itself.

Almond milk: The most common nut-based milk, almond milk has a fairly neutral flavor and aroma. Depending on the ratio of almonds to water, almond milk can have a full body without the need for thickeners. This nondairy milk is easy to make at home and to find in stores.

Cashew milk: With a slightly stronger, nuttier flavor, cashew milk is excellent for cooking and making ice creams. This milk is easy to make at home, though it requires slightly more effort to squeeze in a nut milk bag than almond milk.

Coconut milk: This plant-based milk is sold as a beverage in cartons and in cans for use in cooking. It contains saturated fat, which is considered healthy because the fat is in the form of lauric acid, a medium chain fatty acid that is easily converted to usable energy. Despite its name, coconut milk contains no actual nuts, so it is typically safe for those with a nut allergy (but always consult your physician if you have a life-threatening allergy).

Rice milk: Rice milk has a thinner body and more carbohydrates than other plant-based milks, and is another good alternative for those with a nut allergy.

Soy milk: Of all the plant-based milks, soy milk bears the most nutritional resemblance to dairy milk, with 8 grams of protein per serving. It has a mild aftertaste, however, and many people who are allergic to dairy are also allergic to soy.

1-CUP SERVING	CALORIES	FAT	SATURATED FAT	PROTEIN	CARBOHYDRATES	FIBER
ALMOND MILK	30	2.5g	0g	1g	1g	1g
CASHEW MILK	25	2g	0g	1g	1g	0g
COCONUT MILK (BEVERAGE)	45	4g	3.5g	0g	<1g	0g
COCONUT MILK (CANNED)	420	42g	36g	3g	9g	0g
MACADAMIA MILK	50	5g	1g	1g	1g	1g
OAT MILK	130	2.5g	0g	4g	24g	2g
QUINOA MILK	70	1g	0g	2g	12g	0g
RICE MILK	70	2.5g	0g	0g	11g	0g
SOY MILK	100	4g	0.5g	8g	8g	1g

PART TWO

Recipes

CHAPTER THREE

Plant-Based Milks and Cheeses

Plain or Vanilla Nut Milk

EGG-FREE GLUTEN-FREE VEGAN

MAKES 4 CUPS

PREP TIME:
5 minutes

INGREDIENT TIP: Make the nuts easier to blend and more digestible by soaking them in fresh water for 2 hours or up to overnight before blending. Drain and rinse the soaked nuts thoroughly before proceeding with the recipe.

You can make this nut milk with a variety of nuts—try almonds, Brazil nuts, cashews, or hazelnuts. My go-to nut is almond because the flavor is fairly neutral and almonds are relatively inexpensive. Plain nut milk is a great starting point, and it works better in savory cooking than sweetened vanilla nut milk. Vanilla nut milk is useful in baking, serving over cereal, blending into a smoothie, or just adding to your morning coffee.

1 cup raw unsalted nuts of choice

4 cups water, divided

Pinch sea salt

2 pitted dates or 1 tablespoon maple syrup (use for vanilla nut milk)

1 teaspoon vanilla extract (use for vanilla nut milk)

1. In a blender, combine the nuts, 1 cup of the water, and the salt.

2. **To make vanilla nut milk:** Add the dates and vanilla as well. Puree until very smooth.

3. Add the remaining 3 cups water and blend for 30 seconds. Pour the mixture through a nut milk bag over a large bowl, and squeeze the bag to extract all the liquid.

4. Refrigerate the nut milk in a covered container for up to 5 days. The milk will separate slightly, but simply shake the container to homogenize it again.

PLAIN PER SERVING (1 CUP) Calories: 37; Total Carbohydrates: 2g; Sugar: 0g; Total Fat: 3g; Saturated Fat: 0g; Sodium: 168mg; Protein: 1g; Fiber: 1g

VANILLA PER SERVING (1 CUP) Calories: 53; Total Carbohydrates: 5g; Sugar: 3g; Total Fat: 3g; Saturated Fat: 0g; Sodium: 169mg; Protein: 1g; Fiber: 1g

Cashew Cream

EGG-FREE **GLUTEN-FREE** **VEGAN**

MAKES
1½ CUPS

PREP TIME:
5 minutes, plus
30 minutes
to soak

SERVING TIP:
Blend this
recipe with
1 cup coconut
milk, a splash
of vanilla
extract, and
1 tablespoon
maple syrup
to make a
delicious coffee
creamer.

Cashews are my go-to nut for making a thick, velvety cream. You can use this cream to make baked goods, dairy-free ice cream, and sauces. However, unlike heavy cream, you cannot whip this cashew cream into stiff peaks—for that, use chilled store-bought coconut cream.

1 cup raw unsalted cashews

1½ cups water, divided

Pinch sea salt

1. In a medium bowl, combine the cashews with enough boiling water to cover and leave to soften for 30 minutes. Drain the nuts and rinse until the water runs clear.

2. In a blender, combine the nuts, 1 cup of the water, and the salt. Puree until very smooth.

3. Add the remaining ½ cup water and blend for 30 seconds. Pour the mixture through a nut milk bag over a bowl, and squeeze the bag to extract all the cream.

4. Refrigerate the cream in a covered container for up to 5 days. The cream will separate slightly, but simply shake the container to homogenize it again.

PER SERVING (2 TABLESPOONS) Calories: 80; Total Carbohydrates: 4g; Sugar: 1g; Total Fat: 6g; Saturated Fat: 1g; Sodium: 0mg; Protein: 2g; Fiber: 1g

Soy Milk

EGG-FREE   GLUTEN-FREE   NUT-FREE   VEGAN

MAKES 4 CUPS

PREP TIME:
5 minutes, plus
12 hours
to soak

COOK TIME:
20 minutes

**COOKING
TIP:** To make
a sweetened
vanilla soy milk,
add 1 teaspoon
vanilla extract
and 2 pitted
dates or
1 tablespoon
maple syrup
to the blender
with the soy-
beans in step 2.

Although soy milk is not as easy to make as nut milk, it is a good source of protein and is naturally nut-free. Soybeans (not to be confused with edamame, the young, green soybean) must be cooked to make them digestible, so make sure to heat the blended soybean mixture to at least 180°F and maintain this temperature for the full cooking time.

¾ cup yellow soybeans

4 cups water, divided

Pinch sea salt

1. In a medium bowl, cover the soybeans with 4 cups water and leave to soak for at least 12 hours. Drain the soybeans and rinse until the water runs clear.

2. Remove the soybean skins as thoroughly as possible, then transfer the hulled soybeans to a blender. Add 2 cups of the water and the salt. Blend until mostly smooth.

3. Add the remaining 2 cups water and continue to blend until very smooth. Pour the mixture through a nut milk bag over a bowl, and squeeze the bag to extract all the liquid.

4. Transfer the soy milk to a medium saucepan and bring to a simmer over medium heat. Simmer for 20 minutes, skimming off any foam that rises to the surface.

5. Cool the soy milk completely, then transfer to a covered container. Refrigerate for up to 5 days.

PER SERVING (1 CUP) Calories: 80; Total Carbohydrates: 4g; Sugar: 1g; Total Fat: 4g; Saturated Fat: 1g; Sodium: 85mg; Protein: 7g; Fiber: 1g

Coconut Milk

EGG-FREE **GLUTEN-FREE** **NUT-FREE** **VEGAN**

MAKES 4 CUPS

PREP TIME:
5 minutes

VARIATION TIP:
To make a flavorful toasted coconut milk, toast the coconut in a large dry skillet over medium heat for about 5 minutes, until gently browned, then follow the recipe as directed.

This coconut milk makes a fantastic dairy-free ice cream and can be used in cooking or enjoyed as a delicious beverage. Unlike canned coconut milk found in the grocery store, this version is thinner and does not contain any gums or emulsifiers.

1 cup unsweetened
  coconut flakes

4 cups water, divided

Pinch sea salt

1. In a blender, combine the coconut, 1 cup of the water, and the salt. Puree until very smooth.

2. Add the remaining 3 cups water and blend for at least 30 seconds. Pour the mixture through a nut milk bag over a bowl, and squeeze the bag to extract all the liquid.

3. Refrigerate the coconut milk in a covered container for up to 5 days. The milk will separate slightly, but simply shake the container to homogenize it again.

PER SERVING (1 CUP) Calories: 45; Total Carbohydrates: 1g; Sugar: 1g; Total Fat: 4g; Saturated Fat: 4g; Sodium: 35mg; Protein: 0g; Fiber: 0g

Rice or Quinoa Milk

ALLERGEN-FREE   EGG-FREE   GLUTEN-FREE   NUT-FREE   VEGAN

MAKES 4 CUPS

PREP TIME:
5 minutes

**INGREDIENT
TIP:** If you have
leftover rice
or quinoa but
don't want to
make milk right
away, you can
store the grains
in a resealable
bag in the
freezer for up
to 3 months.

SERVING TIP:
Transform the
rice milk into
a delicious
Mexican-
inspired
horchata
by adding
½ teaspoon
ground
cinnamon,
½ teaspoon
vanilla
extract, and
2 tablespoons
brown sugar or
maple syrup.

Once you realize how easy it is to make homemade milk, you'll know exactly what to do with that leftover takeout container of rice—milk it! You can use either white or brown rice in this recipe. Quinoa is an excellent source of protein and makes a more strongly flavored milk, which is especially good blended into smoothies or used as a liquid in baking.

1 cup cooked rice or quinoa   Pinch sea salt

4 cups water, divided

1. In a blender, combine the rice, 1 cup of the water, and the salt. Puree until very smooth.

2. Add the remaining 3 cups water, and blend for 30 seconds. Pour the mixture through a nut milk bag over a bowl, and squeeze the bag to extract all the liquid.

3. Refrigerate the milk in a covered container for up to 5 days. The milk will separate slightly, but simply shake the container to homogenize it again.

RICE MILK PER SERVING (1 CUP) Calories: 65; Total Carbohydrates: 11g; Sugar: 1g; Total Fat: 2g; Saturated Fat: 0g; Sodium: 110mg; Protein: 0g; Fiber: 0g

QUINOA MILK PER SERVING (1 CUP) Calories: 70; Total Carbohydrates: 12g; Sugar: 2g; Total Fat: 1g; Saturated Fat: 0g; Sodium: 0mg; Protein: 2g; Fiber: 0g

Plant-Based Parmesan

EGG-FREE   GLUTEN-FREE   VEGAN

MAKES 1 CUP

PREP TIME:
5 minutes

COOKING TIP:
When blending
the Parmesan,
a clean coffee
grinder does
a nice job. To
avoid over-
crowding the
machine, blend
in batches.

I know it's culinary sacrilege, but I once actually liked those green cans of Parmesan. There was something about the dry, salty bits showered over pizza or pasta that just worked for me. Fortunately, the dairy-free version of canned Parmesan is easier to replicate than aged Parmesan wedges.

1 cup raw unsalted cashews

¼ cup nutritional yeast

1 teaspoon sea salt

1 teaspoon garlic powder

1. In a small food processor, combine the cashews, nutritional yeast, salt, and garlic powder. Pulse until finely ground.

2. Transfer the mixture to a covered container and store at room temperature indefinitely.

PER SERVING (2 TABLESPOONS) Calories: 109; Total Carbohydrates: 8g; Sugar: 0g; Total Fat: 6g; Saturated Fat: 1g; Sodium: 234mg; Protein: 7g; Fiber: 3g

Basic Nut Cheese

EGG-FREE GLUTEN-FREE VEGAN

MAKES
1¼ CUPS

PREP TIME:
5 minutes,
plus
30 minutes
to soak

SERVING TIP:
To make a
scrumptious
spreadable
cheese, stir in
1 tablespoon
minced
shallot and
1 tablespoon
minced fresh
herbs, such as
basil, rosemary,
or tarragon.

You can make this nut cheese with blanched almonds, cashews, or macadamia nuts. It works beautifully in dairy-free lasagna, crêpes, or other recipes where ricotta cheese is called for. It's especially important to soak the nuts before blending, otherwise you'll need to add too much water to get the blender going.

1 cup raw unsalted nuts

2 cups boiling water

½ cup water, divided

2 tablespoons freshly squeezed lemon juice

¾ teaspoon sea salt

1. In a medium bowl, cover the nuts with the boiling water and leave to soak for 30 minutes. Alternatively, cover them with cold water and soak overnight. Drain the nuts and rinse until the water runs clear.

2. In a blender, combine the nuts, ¼ cup of the water, the lemon juice, and salt. Puree until mostly smooth, adding more water if necessary (you might not need it all).

3. Transfer the nut cheese to a covered container and refrigerate for up to 5 days. The cheese will separate slightly, but simply shake the container to homogenize it again.

PER SERVING (¼ CUP) Calories: 126; Total Carbohydrates: 6g; Sugar: 0g; Total Fat: 10g; Saturated Fat: 2g; Sodium: 73mg; Protein: 4g; Fiber: 1g

Tofu Ricotta

EGG-FREE GLUTEN-FREE NUT-FREE VEGAN

MAKES 2 CUPS

PREP TIME:
10 minutes

INGREDIENT TIP: The quality of the tofu you use really does matter for flavor here. I use Wildwood brand organic sprouted tofu.

VARIATION TIP: To make a sweet tofu ricotta, omit the garlic and reduce the salt to ½ teaspoon.

I use the Basic Nut Cheese (page 28) and this tofu ricotta interchangeably when making Lasagna (page 137). This version is lighter in texture than regular ricotta but has a great flavor. Also, don't be tempted to skip the sugar in the recipe; milk contains naturally occurring sugars, so adding sugar to the tofu is essential to re-creating a similar flavor.

1 (14-ounce) package firm tofu, drained and broken into pieces

¼ cup extra-virgin olive oil

2½ tablespoons freshly squeezed lemon juice

2 teaspoons sugar

1 teaspoon minced garlic

1 teaspoon sea salt

1. In a food processor, combine the tofu, oil, lemon juice, sugar, garlic, and salt. Blend until mostly smooth.

2. Transfer to a covered container and refrigerate for up to 5 days. The ricotta will separate slightly, but simply shake the container to homogenize it again.

PER SERVING (¼ CUP) Calories: 94; Total Carbohydrates: 2g; Sugar: 1g; Total Fat: 8g; Saturated Fat: 1g; Sodium: 241mg; Protein: 4g; Fiber: 1g

CHAPTER FOUR

Smoothies and Breakfast

Creamy Banana-Almond Protein Shake

EGG-FREE GLUTEN-FREE MAKE ALLERGEN-FREE MAKE NUT-FREE VEGAN

SERVES 1

PREP TIME:
5 minutes

INGREDIENT TIP: My favorite plant-based protein powders are the sport versions of Vega and Garden of Life in chocolate flavor. These are sweetened with stevia, contain up to 30 grams of protein per serving, and don't contain soy.

SUBSTITUTION TIP: To make this allergen-free and nut-free, use Rice or Quinoa Milk (page 26) instead of the Vanilla Nut Milk.

This is my favorite breakfast. I drink one of these shakes nearly every single day, especially on busy mornings when I want to sneak in a workout before rushing the kids off to school and heading to work. It's cool, creamy, and packed with plant-based protein. I highly recommend freezing the diced banana ahead for especially thick and creamy results.

1 medium banana, diced, frozen

1 cup Vanilla Nut Milk (page 22), made with almonds, or store-bought unsweetened almond milk

1 cup ice, divided

1 scoop chocolate dairy-free protein powder (see Ingredient Tip)

1. In a blender, combine the banana, nut milk, and ½ cup of the ice. Pulse until mostly smooth, adding more ice as desired.

2. Add the protein powder and blend until smooth, stopping to scrape down the sides of the blender with a spatula as needed.

PER SERVING Calories: 285; Total Carbohydrates: 41g; Sugar: 16g; Total Fat: 7g; Saturated Fat: 1g; Sodium: 311mg; Protein: 16g; Fiber: 11g

Green Monster Smoothie

ALLERGEN-FREE **EGG-FREE** **GLUTEN-FREE** **NUT-FREE** **VEGAN**

SERVES 1

PREP TIME:
10 minutes

INGREDIENT TIP: To peel the lime, cut off each end with a sharp knife, then stand it on one end and cut away the outer peel.

I introduced this smoothie to my boys at an early age, and they quickly slurped it down. It's a convenient way to serve them dark leafy greens while they're still a little suspicious of salads. To make this smoothie a complete meal, serve with a handful of nuts or a healthy protein bar.

1 cup firmly packed kale or fresh spinach

1 lime, peeled

1 small banana, peeled

½ cup frozen diced pineapple

Small handful fresh cilantro (optional)

Small handful fresh parsley (optional)

¼ to ½ cup water

In a blender, combine the kale, lime, banana, pineapple, cilantro (if using), and parsley (if using). Puree until very smooth, adding just enough water to blend.

PER SERVING Calories: 199; Total Carbohydrates: 52g; Sugar: 24g; Total Fat: 1g; Saturated Fat: 0g; Sodium: 33mg; Protein: 4g; Fiber: 7g

Piña Colada Smoothie

ALLERGEN-FREE EGG-FREE GLUTEN-FREE NUT-FREE VEGAN

SERVES 1

PREP TIME:
5 minutes

VARIATION TIP:
If you want to
turn this into
a grown-up
drink, who am
I to stop you?
Add 3 ounces
white rum
and divide the
smoothie into
two portions.

Close your eyes and let this tropical treat deliver you to a faraway place. This virgin breakfast smoothie is filled with complex carbs and healthy fats from the coconut milk. For added nutrition, include a scoop of vanilla protein powder.

1 cup Coconut Milk (page 25)   1 small banana, diced, frozen
Juice of ½ lime   1 cup frozen diced pineapple

In a blender, combine the coconut milk, lime juice, banana, and pineapple. Puree until smooth.

PER SERVING Calories: 238; Total Carbohydrates: 53g; Sugar: 31g; Total Fat: 5g; Saturated Fat: 4g; Sodium: 4mg; Protein: 2g; Fiber: 7g

Apple Pie Oatmeal

EGG-FREE GLUTEN-FREE MAKE ALLERGEN-FREE MAKE NUT-FREE VEGAN

SERVES 4

PREP TIME:
10 minutes

COOK TIME:
5 minutes

**SUBSTITUTION
TIP:** To
make this
allergen-free,
use soy-free
dairy-free
butter, omit the
pecans, and
use a nut- and
soy-free milk.

My kids adore hot cereal for breakfast, especially this quick and easy apple pie oatmeal with all the flavors of the classic dessert. This dish takes just a few minutes longer to prepare than an instant oatmeal packet, but contains a fraction of the sugar.

2 cups old-fashioned oats

2 apples, peeled,
    cored, and diced

1 teaspoon ground cinnamon

1 teaspoon vanilla extract

¼ teaspoon sea salt

4½ cups water

4 teaspoons brown sugar

4 teaspoons dairy-free
    butter (such as Earth
    Balance Buttery Spread)

4 tablespoons finely chopped
    pecans (optional)

4 tablespoons Vanilla
    Nut Milk (page 22)

1. In a large saucepan, stir together the oats, apples, cinnamon, vanilla, salt, and water and bring to a simmer over medium heat. Cover the pan, reduce the heat to low, and simmer for 5 minutes.

2. Divide the oatmeal among four serving bowls. Top each with 1 teaspoon of the brown sugar, 1 teaspoon of the butter, 1 tablespoon of the pecans (if using), and 1 tablespoon of the nut milk.

PER SERVING Calories: 158; Total Carbohydrates: 23g; Sugar: 7g; Total Fat: 7g; Saturated Fat: 1g; Sodium: 167mg; Protein: 3g; Fiber: 3g

Creamy Oatmeal with Caramelized Bananas

EGG-FREE   GLUTEN-FREE   MAKE ALLERGEN-FREE   MAKE NUT-FREE   VEGAN

SERVES 4

PREP TIME:
10 minutes

COOK TIME:
10 minutes

SUBSTITUTION TIP: To make this nut-free and allergen-free, substitute additional coconut milk for the nut milk and omit the hazelnuts.

INGREDIENT TIP: If you're short on time and want to ditch some of the fat and sugar in this recipe, skip caramelizing the bananas and just serve raw banana slices on the oatmeal. It's still delicious!

If your morning oatmeal has become a predictable routine, change it up with this recipe for a real treat! This creamy, decadent breakfast borders on dessert and is a good fit for the weekend. The caramelized bananas are a cinch to make, so you can serve this dish any day of the week.

2 cups old-fashioned rolled oats

2 cups Coconut Milk (page 25)

2 cups Plain Nut Milk (page 22), made with almonds

¼ teaspoon sea salt

1 tablespoon vanilla extract

1 tablespoon coconut oil or canola oil

2 medium bananas, cut into ½-inch-thick slices

1 tablespoon brown sugar

4 teaspoons dairy-free butter (such as Earth Balance Buttery Spread)

4 tablespoons finely chopped toasted hazelnuts

1. In a large saucepan, stir together the oats, coconut milk, nut milk, salt, and vanilla and bring to a simmer over medium heat.

2. Cover the pan, reduce the heat to low, and simmer for 5 minutes.

3. While the oatmeal cooks, in a large skillet over medium-high heat, heat the oil.

4. Sprinkle the banana slices on both sides with brown sugar. Arrange the bananas in a single layer in the skillet and cook for about 2 minutes, until nicely caramelized but not blackened. Flip the bananas carefully and cook for 2 minutes more.

5. To serve, divide the cooked oatmeal among four serving bowls, top with the caramelized bananas, then top each serving with 1 teaspoon of the butter and 1 tablespoon of the hazelnuts.

PER SERVING Calories: 364; Total Carbohydrates: 29g; Sugar: 8g; Total Fat: 26g; Saturated Fat: 10g; Sodium: 463mg; Protein: 4g; Fiber: 5g

French Toast

SERVES 4

PREP TIME:
5 minutes

COOK TIME:
30 minutes

SUBSTITUTION TIP: To make this nut-free, substitute another plant-based milk for the nut milk and omit the sliced almonds.

VARIATION TIP: For extra richness, use Cashew Cream (page 23) in the batter instead of nut milk.

French toast, a timeless decadence, is easily made dairy-free using Vanilla Nut Milk (page 22), but you can try any plant-based milk in this recipe. If you opt for an unsweetened milk, add a splash of vanilla extract and maple syrup to the batter.

3 tablespoons coconut oil or canola oil, divided

2 large eggs

1 cup Vanilla Nut Milk (page 22)

½ teaspoon ground cinnamon

10 slices wheat bread or gluten-free bread

1 cup fresh berries (such as blueberries or raspberries)

2 tablespoons powdered sugar

2 tablespoons sliced almonds, toasted

4 teaspoons dairy-free butter (such as Earth Balance Buttery Spread)

1. Preheat the oven to 350°F. Coat the interior of a 9-by-13-inch casserole dish with 1 tablespoon of the oil.

2. In a wide, shallow bowl, whisk the eggs, nut milk, and cinnamon to blend.

3. Dredge the bread slices in the egg mixture and arrange them in the prepared casserole dish, overlapping them slightly. Spread the berries over the toast.

4. Bake for 25 to 30 minutes, until golden brown.

5. Shower the French toast with the powdered sugar and top with the sliced almonds. Serve with the butter.

PER SERVING Calories: 408; Total Carbohydrates: 42g; Sugar: 13g; Total Fat: 22g; Saturated Fat: 8g; Sodium: 397mg; Protein: 11g; Fiber: 4g

Lemon–Olive Oil Breakfast Cakes with Berry Syrup

GLUTEN-FREE **VEGETARIAN**

SERVES 4

PREP TIME:
5 minutes

COOK TIME:
10 minutes

Olive oil–based cakes are common in the Mediterranean, and are satisfyingly rich.

FOR THE PANCAKES

1 cup almond flour

1 teaspoon baking powder

¼ teaspoon salt

6 tablespoons extra-virgin
  olive oil, divided

2 large eggs

Grated zest and juice of 1 lemon

½ teaspoon almond or
  vanilla extract

FOR THE BERRY SYRUP

1 cup frozen mixed berries

1 tablespoon water or freshly
  squeezed lemon juice,
  plus more as needed

½ teaspoon vanilla extract

1. **To make the pancakes:** In a large bowl, whisk the almond flour, baking powder, and salt to break up any clumps.

2. Add 4 tablespoons of the oil, the eggs, lemon zest and juice, and almond extract and whisk well to combine.

3. In a large skillet over medium heat, warm 1 tablespoon of the oil. Spoon 2 tablespoons of the batter into the skillet. Cook for 4 to 5 minutes, until bubbles begin to form, then flip. Cook for 2 to 3 minutes on the second side. Transfer to a plate. Repeat with the remaining oil and batter.

4. **To make the berry syrup:** In a small saucepan, mix the frozen berries, water, and vanilla. Heat over medium-high heat for 3 to 4 minutes, until bubbly, adding more water if the mixture is too thick. Mash the berries and whisk until smooth.

5. Serve the pancakes with the warm berry syrup.

PER SERVING Calories: 377; Total Carbohydrates: 11g; Sugar: 3g; Total Fat: 35g; Saturated Fat: 4g; Sodium: 183mg; Protein: 9g; Fiber: 5g

Waffles with Strawberries and Whipped Cream

NUT-FREE **VEGETARIAN**

SERVES 4

PREP TIME:
10 minutes

COOK TIME:
15 minutes

Doesn't this recipe sound luscious? It is! I've found that the protein and fat in soy milk mimic dairy milk more closely and that soy milk works better in this recipe than other plant-based milks. Waffles are usually made with butter, which provides the crisp texture that makes them so delectable, but I've opted for coconut or canola oil here. Melted dairy-free butter also works.

1¼ cups all-purpose flour

1 tablespoon sugar

1½ teaspoons baking powder

½ teaspoon sea salt

1 cup Soy Milk (page 24)

⅓ cup coconut oil or canola oil, plus 1 teaspoon

1 large egg, whisked

1 pint fresh strawberries, hulled and thinly sliced

1 cup Coconut Whipped Cream (page 167)

1. Preheat the oven to 200°F.

2. In a medium bowl, combine the flour, sugar, baking powder, and salt. Whisk in the soy milk, ⅓ cup of the oil, and egg until just combined.

3. Preheat the waffle iron. Brush with some of the remaining 1 teaspoon oil.

4. Pour about ½ cup of the batter (depending on the waffle maker's size, more or less batter may be needed) into the waffle iron. Cook until browned, place on an oven-safe dish, and transfer to the oven to keep warm.

5. Repeat with the remaining batter, adding more oil to the waffle iron between batches as needed.

6. To serve, place a waffle on a serving plate and top with a generous heap of strawberries and a spoonful of whipped cream.

PER SERVING Calories: 443; Total Carbohydrates: 42g; Sugar: 8g; Total Fat: 28g; Saturated Fat: 22g; Sodium: 333mg; Protein: 8g; Fiber: 3g

Creamy Vegetable Strata

MAKE GLUTEN-FREE MAKE NUT-FREE VEGETARIAN

SERVES 6

PREP TIME:
10 minutes

COOK TIME:
25 minutes

**INGREDIENT
TIP:** If you're
using store-
bought milk,
make sure it
is plain and
unsweet-
ened. Sweet,
vanilla-flavored
milk doesn't
work in
this savory
casserole.

This hearty breakfast casserole is loaded with flavor and complex carbohydrates. Use whatever vegetables you have on hand—just make sure they're precooked or safe to eat after minimal cooking. When the strata bakes, it warms and softens the vegetables, but there is insufficient time to cook some foods (for example, raw potatoes).

1 tablespoon canola oil

8 large eggs

1 cup Plain Nut Milk (page 22) or Soy Milk (page 24)

½ teaspoon sea salt

¼ teaspoon freshly ground black pepper

2 slices wheat or gluten-free bread, crusts removed, cubed, and toasted

1 (8-ounce) container dairy-free cream cheese, cubed (optional)

1 cup frozen broccoli, thawed

½ cup frozen corn, thawed

1 red bell pepper, finely diced

2 tablespoons minced fresh basil or parsley

1. Preheat the oven to 400°F. Coat the interior of a 2-quart casserole dish with the oil.

2. In a large measuring cup, whisk the eggs, nut milk, salt, and pepper to blend.

3. Spread the toasted bread cubes, cream cheese (if using), broccoli, corn, bell pepper, and basil in the prepared casserole dish. Pour the egg mixture over the top, and gently stir to evenly distribute the ingredients.

4. Bake, uncovered, for 20 to 25 minutes, until the eggs are set and the top is lightly browned. Let rest for 5 minutes before serving.

PER SERVING Calories: 159; Total Carbohydrates: 10g; Sugar: 2g; Total Fat: 9g; Saturated Fat: 2g; Sodium: 320mg; Protein: 10g; Fiber: 2g

Fluffy Biscuits and Sausage Gravy

EGG-FREE   **MAKE GLUTEN-FREE**   **NUT-FREE**

SERVES 4

PREP TIME:
15 minutes

COOK TIME:
15 minutes

INGREDIENT
TIP: For even
better results,
freeze the
butter in small
cubes, which
keeps it from
fully mixing
into the biscuit
dough and
produces a
flakier biscuit.

Forgive me. This isn't exactly health food, but sometimes you just crave fluffy biscuits and creamy, rich sausage gravy. The lemon juice might sound strange in the biscuits, but go with me. It reacts with the baking soda to leaven the biscuits.

FOR THE BISCUITS

1 cup all-purpose flour or gluten-free flour blend, plus more for dusting

2 teaspoons aluminum-free baking powder

¼ teaspoon baking soda

½ teaspoon sea salt

4 tablespoons (½ stick) very cold dairy-free butter (such as Earth Balance Buttery Spread), cut into small cubes

1 teaspoon freshly squeezed lemon juice

⅓ cup Plain Nut Milk (page 22)

FOR THE GRAVY

8 ounces garlic pork sausage, casings removed, crumbled

2 tablespoons all-purpose flour or gluten-free flour blend

1½ cups Soy Milk (page 24)

Sea salt

Freshly ground black pepper

1. **To make the biscuits:** Preheat the oven to 425°F. Line a sheet pan with parchment paper.

2. In a food processor, combine the flour, baking powder, baking soda, and salt. Add the butter and pulse until small chunks remain.

3. Stir the lemon juice into the nut milk and pour the milk into the food processor. Pulse once or twice, stopping to scrape down the sides of the processor as needed, just until the dough comes together.

4. Dust a clean work surface with flour, then transfer the dough to the floured surface. Gently pat the dough into a large circle or rectangle ¾- to 1-inch thick.

5. Use a round drinking glass or cookie cutter to cut the dough into biscuits and transfer them to the prepared sheet pan. Gently reshape the dough scraps to cut more biscuits from and repeat until all the dough is used. You should have about four biscuits.

6. Bake for 12 to 14 minutes, until the biscuits are gently browned and puffy.

7. **To make the gravy:** While the biscuits bake, heat a large skillet over medium heat. Add the sausage and cook for about 5 minutes, until lightly browned and just cooked through.

8. Sprinkle the flour over the sausage. With a wooden spoon, scrape up the browned bits from the bottom of the skillet. Cook for about 1 minute, or until the flour has absorbed the fat.

9. Pour in the soy milk and season to taste with salt and pepper. Cook, stirring frequently, until the gravy is thickened and bubbling. Remove from the heat.

10. To serve, halve the biscuits and top each with a generous spoonful of gravy.

PER SERVING Calories: 449; Total Carbohydrates: 30g; Sugar: 1g; Total Fat: 30g; Saturated Fat: 13g; Sodium: 964mg; Protein: 15g; Fiber: 3g

Tex-Mex Breakfast Burritos

MAKE GLUTEN-FREE NUT-FREE VEGETARIAN

SERVES 4

PREP TIME:
10 minutes

COOK TIME:
10 minutes

**SUBSTITUTION
TIP:** To make
this recipe
gluten-free,
purchase
gluten-free
flour tortillas.
Corn tortillas
are okay, too,
but they are
smaller and
should be
warmed first
to prevent
cracking when
folding.

As its name suggests, Tex-Mex is a fusion of Texan and Mexican cuisines, characterized by heavy use of shredded cheese, beans, ground meat, sautéed onions and peppers, and spices. This version skips the cheese and meat for a healthy, flavorful, veggie-packed breakfast burrito.

1 tablespoon canola oil

1 green bell pepper, thinly sliced

1 small yellow onion, halved
  and thinly sliced

1 teaspoon ground cumin

Sea salt

Freshly ground black pepper

6 large eggs, whisked

4 (10-inch) flour tortillas

1 cup canned chili beans,
  drained, warmed

2 tablespoons minced
  fresh cilantro

¼ cup Dairy-Free Sour Cream
  (page 173) or store-bought
  dairy-free sour cream

½ cup guacamole

Hot sauce (such as
  Cholula), for serving

1. In a large skillet over medium-high heat, heat the oil. Add the bell pepper and onion and sauté for about 5 minutes, until lightly browned and soft. Stir in the cumin. Season generously with salt and pepper. Transfer to a dish.

2. Return the skillet to the heat and cook the eggs for 2 to 3 minutes just until set.

3. To assemble the burritos, place the tortillas on a work surface. Evenly divide the chili beans, sautéed pepper and onion, eggs, and cilantro among the flour tortillas.

4. Top each with 1 tablespoon of the sour cream and 2 tablespoons of the guacamole. Season with hot sauce, as desired. Fold into a burrito and enjoy immediately.

PER SERVING Calories: 380; Total Carbohydrates: 34g; Sugar: 6g; Total Fat: 22g; Saturated Fat: 4g; Sodium: 657mg; Protein: 15g; Fiber: 8g

Farmers' Market Hash

GLUTEN-FREE **NUT-FREE** **VEGETARIAN**

SERVES 4

PREP TIME:
15 minutes

COOK TIME:
45 minutes

When making this hash, use whatever vegetables are in season. If you don't have sriracha, use another hot sauce, such as Cholula or Tapatío.

2 russet potatoes, scrubbed and diced

2 small sweet potatoes, scrubbed and diced

1 red bell pepper, sliced

1 yellow onion, halved and sliced

1 rosemary sprig, leaves removed and minced

4 tablespoons canola oil, divided

Sea salt

Freshly ground black pepper

1 large tomato, cut into large chunks

4 large eggs

Large handful fresh basil leaves

Sriracha, for serving

1. Preheat the oven to 375°F. Line a sheet pan with parchment paper.

2. Spread the russet potatoes, sweet potatoes, bell pepper, onion, and rosemary on the pan and drizzle with 3 tablespoons of the oil. Using your hands, gently toss to coat. Season with salt and pepper.

3. Roast, uncovered, for 30 minutes, or until the vegetables are tender and begin to brown on the bottom.

4. Add the tomato to the pan and roast for 5 to 10 minutes, until the tomato has shrunken somewhat.

5. Meanwhile, heat a large skillet over medium-high heat. Once hot, heat the remaining 1 tablespoon oil for about 15 seconds until hot.

6. Crack the eggs into the skillet, being careful not to break the yolks. Season with salt and pepper. Cook for 5 to 7 minutes, until the whites are set and browned around the edges.

7. Meanwhile, stack the basil leaves and roll them into a tight cylinder. Using a sharp knife, thinly slice across the basil roll to make a chiffonade. Scatter the basil over the cooked vegetables.

8. To serve, divide the roasted vegetables among four serving dishes and top each with a fried egg. Serve with sriracha.

PER SERVING Calories: 432; Total Carbohydrates: 57g; Sugar: 7g; Total Fat: 19g; Saturated Fat: 3g; Sodium: 142mg; Protein: 11g; Fiber: 9g

Blueberry Coffee Cake

MAKE GLUTEN-FREE **VEGETARIAN**

SERVES 6

PREP TIME:
10 minutes

COOK TIME:
40 minutes

VARIATION TIP:
Turn this dish
into a classic
coffee cake by
omitting the
blueberries and
lemon zest.
Add 1 teaspoon
ground cin-
namon to the
cake batter and
½ teaspoon
ground
cinnamon to
the streusel
topping.

This fruit-studded coffee cake is perfect for a lazy midmorning brunch or afternoon tea. If fresh blueberries aren't available, use frozen berries or another fruit, such as peaches.

Juice of 1 lemon

½ cup Vanilla Nut Milk (page 22)

12 tablespoons (1½ sticks) dairy-free butter (such as Earth Balance Buttery Spread), at room temperature, divided

½ cup sugar, plus 2 tablespoons

2 large eggs, whisked

1 teaspoon vanilla extract

Grated zest of 1 lemon

2 cups all-purpose flour or gluten-free flour blend, plus 2 tablespoons

2 teaspoons baking powder

1 teaspoon sea salt

2 cups fresh blueberries

¼ cup old-fashioned rolled oats

1. Preheat the oven to 350°F. Line an 8-by-8-inch baking dish with parchment paper.

2. In a small bowl, stir together the lemon juice and nut milk. Set aside to make a mock buttermilk.

3. In a large bowl, beat 8 tablespoons (1 stick) of butter with ½ cup of the sugar until thick and fluffy. Add the eggs, vanilla, and lemon zest and beat for about 30 seconds just until integrated.

4. Sift in the flour, baking powder, and salt. Stir in the lemon–nut milk mixture just until integrated. Small lumps will remain. Fold in the blueberries. Pour the mixture into the prepared baking dish.

5. In a small bowl, stir together the remaining 4 tablespoons (½ stick) butter, remaining 2 tablespoons sugar, remaining 2 tablespoons flour, and the oats. Sprinkle this streusel over the cake.

6. Bake for 40 minutes, or until a cake tester inserted into the center of the coffee cake comes out clean.

PER SERVING Calories: 494; Total Carbohydrates: 62g; Sugar: 26g; Total Fat: 25g; Saturated Fat: 7g; Sodium: 572mg; Protein: 7g; Fiber: 3g

Coconut-Mango Porridge

EGG-FREE **GLUTEN-FREE** **VEGAN**

SERVES 4

PREP TIME:
5 minutes, plus
30 minutes
to soak plus
2 hours to chill

Looking for something a little different? This breakfast pudding has all the taste of the tropics. It also makes a delicious snack or dessert. Prepare it the night before so it's ready when you wake up.

½ cup raw unsalted cashews, soaked in hot water for at least 30 minutes

½ cup unsweetened shredded coconut

1 cup lite coconut milk, divided

¼ cup water

2 tablespoons maple syrup, plus more as desired

2 tablespoons freshly squeezed lime juice

Pinch sea salt

2 tablespoons coconut oil

2 cups diced mango

1. Drain and rinse the cashews, put them in a blender, and add the coconut and ½ cup of the coconut milk. Blend until smooth, adding only as much water as needed to keep the blender moving.

2. When the cashews are completely smooth, add the remaining ½ cup coconut milk, the maple syrup, lime juice, and salt.

3. With the motor running, pour in the oil and blend until thoroughly integrated. Divide the mixture among four small ramekins or glass jars.

4. Clean the blender thoroughly, then add the mango and puree until smooth. Pour over the coconut puddings. Chill for 2 hours before serving.

PER SERVING Calories: 428; Total Carbohydrates: 32g; Sugar: 21g; Total Fat: 34g; Saturated Fat: 29g; Sodium: 75mg; Protein: 4g; Fiber: 7g

Salads and Soups

Caesar Salad

SERVES 4

PREP TIME:
5 minutes

SUBSTITUTION TIP: To make an egg-free and allergen-free version of this salad dressing, use a blend of vegan mayonnaise and vegan Worcestershire sauce.

A dairy-free Caesar salad is easier to make than you might think. Preparing the dressing from scratch allows you to omit the dairy Parmesan and enjoy a safe and healthy Caesar. Top it with Plant-Based Parmesan (page 27) some croutons for a little crunch.

3 garlic cloves, minced

1 teaspoon anchovy paste

1 teaspoon Worcestershire sauce

½ teaspoon Dijon mustard

1 tablespoon freshly squeezed lemon juice

⅓ cup mayonnaise

2 tablespoons extra-virgin olive oil

Sea salt

Freshly ground black pepper

2 heads romaine lettuce, roughly chopped

1 cup croutons (optional)

¼ cup Plant-Based Parmesan (page 27; optional)

1. In a large bowl, whisk the garlic, anchovy paste, Worcestershire sauce, mustard, lemon juice, and mayonnaise to blend. Slowly drizzle in the oil, whisking constantly. Season with salt and pepper.

2. Add the romaine lettuce to the bowl and use tongs to toss the salad until well coated. Before serving, top with the croutons (if using) and Parmesan (if using).

PER SERVING Calories: 188; Total Carbohydrates: 13g; Sugar: 3g; Total Fat: 14g; Saturated Fat: 2g; Sodium: 300mg; Protein: 4g; Fiber: 1g

Peanut-Ginger Cold Pasta Salad

EGG-FREE   MAKE GLUTEN-FREE   VEGAN

SERVES 4

PREP TIME:
10 minutes

COOK TIME:
10 minutes

INGREDIENT TIP: For a different spin, use cashew or almond butter instead of peanut butter and top the dish with roughly chopped roasted cashews.

SUBSTITUTION TIP: To make this dish gluten-free, use gluten-free soy sauce and noodles.

This is one of my family's favorite summertime dinners. The sweet and spicy dressing coats the chilled noodles and crunchy vegetables and pleases the palate. Add chicken, tofu, or another protein to make this a complete meal.

12 ounces spaghetti noodles

¼ cup soy sauce

Juice of 2 limes

1 tablespoon natural peanut butter

1 teaspoon minced peeled fresh ginger

1 teaspoon minced garlic

1 teaspoon sambal oelek, or pinch red pepper flakes

1 teaspoon maple syrup or honey

1 small cucumber, peeled, seeded, and diced

1 cup sugar snap peas, stringed and halved

½ cup roughly chopped fresh mint

½ cup roughly chopped fresh cilantro

½ cup toasted peanuts, roughly chopped

1. Cook the spaghetti according to the package directions, being careful not to overcook them. Drain the noodles and rinse under cool running water. Drain thoroughly.

2. In a small lidded jar, combine the soy sauce, lime juice, peanut butter, ginger, garlic, sambal oelek, and maple syrup. Seal the jar tightly and vigorously shake the dressing to combine.

3. In a serving bowl, combine the chilled noodles, cucumber, snap peas, mint, and cilantro. Drizzle with the dressing and gently toss to coat.

4. Before serving, top the salad with the toasted peanuts.

PER SERVING Calories: 488; Total Carbohydrates: 78g; Sugar: 8g; Total Fat: 13g; Saturated Fat: 2g; Sodium: 910mg; Protein: 18g; Fiber: 7g

Southwestern Chicken Salad with Chipotle Ranch

SERVES 4

PREP TIME:
15 minutes

COOK TIME:
10 minutes

SERVING TIP:
For a little crunch, top each salad with 1 tablespoon toasted pepitas (pumpkin seeds).

This entrée salad is perfect for dinner or a nice lunch. Each component can be prepared ahead for easy assembly later. I love the chipotle ranch—it is perfectly creamy, spicy, and addicting.

2 (6-ounce) boneless, skinless chicken breasts

1 teaspoon smoked paprika

1 teaspoon ground cumin

Sea salt

Freshly ground black pepper

1 tablespoon canola oil

1 head romaine lettuce, roughly chopped

¼ cup roughly chopped fresh cilantro

1 cup canned black beans, drained and rinsed

1 large tomato, diced

1 avocado, peeled, halved, pitted, and thinly sliced

1 cup frozen corn, thawed

1 to 2 teaspoons minced chipotle pepper in adobo

½ cup Ranch Dressing (page 170)

1. Between two pieces of parchment or wax paper, pound the chicken breasts to a uniform ½-inch thickness. Season the chicken with paprika, cumin, salt, and pepper.

2. In a large skillet over medium-high heat, heat the oil until hot. Add the chicken to the skillet and sear for about 4 minutes per side, or until lightly browned and cooked to 160°F. Transfer to a cutting board to rest.

3. To assemble the salad, evenly divide the romaine lettuce, cilantro, black beans, tomato, avocado, and corn among four serving bowls.

4. In a small bowl, whisk 1 teaspoon of the chipotle into the ranch dressing, adding more chipotle as desired for a spicier dressing.

5. Cut the chicken breasts into thin strips and lay them on the salads. Drizzle each salad with chipotle ranch.

PER SERVING Calories: 343; Total Carbohydrates: 27g; Sugar: 4g; Total Fat: 16g; Saturated Fat: 3g; Sodium: 381mg; Protein: 27g; Fiber: 10g

Strawberry-Spinach Salad

EGG-FREE GLUTEN-FREE VEGAN

SERVES 4

PREP TIME:
10 minutes

COOKING TIP:
This recipe
makes 1 cup
balsamic
vinaigrette—
more than you
will need to
dress the salad.
Preparing the
dressing in
a jar with a
lid makes for
easy storage;
refrigerate left-
overs for up to
5 days and give
the jar a good
shake before
serving again.

**SUBSTITUTION
TIP:** If you're
short on time
but want the
creamy nut
cheese, opt for
a store-bought
variety, such
as Treeline
or Miyoko's
Creamery.

Cool, creamy, soft cheese is a wonderful complement to many green salads. Fortunately, nut cheese works really well in place of goat cheese, feta, and other soft cheeses. It serves as the "icing on the cake" for this colorful and healthy salad.

FOR THE DRESSING

1 shallot, minced

1 tablespoon minced fresh basil

⅓ cup balsamic vinegar

⅔ cup extra-virgin olive oil

1 teaspoon maple syrup

Sea salt

Freshly ground black pepper

FOR THE SALAD

8 cups fresh baby spinach

1 pint fresh strawberries, hulled and sliced

½ small red onion, thinly sliced

½ cup Basic Nut Cheese (page 28), broken into bite-size chunks

1. **To make the dressing:** In a small, lidded jar, combine the shallot, basil, vinegar, oil, maple syrup, salt, and pepper. Cover the jar tightly and shake until the dressing is emulsified.

2. **To assemble the salad:** In a large bowl, combine the spinach, straw-berries, and red onion. Add ¼ cup of the dressing, gently tossing to coat the leaves in the dressing.

3. Divide the salad among four plates.

4. Sprinkle the nut cheese over the salad. Serve immediately.

PER SERVING Calories: 115; Total Carbohydrates: 11g; Sugar: 6g; Total Fat: 7g; Saturated Fat: 1g; Sodium: 184mg; Protein: 3g; Fiber: 4g

The Waldorf Salad

GLUTEN-FREE VEGAN

SERVES 4

PREP TIME:
10 minutes

**INGREDIENT
TIP:** I use a
Medjool date
to add a hint
of sweetness,
which balances
the tangy sour
cream, but
any type of
date or dried
fruit will do.

Dairy-free sour cream brings delightful richness to this fruit-and-veggie-forward salad. Using a fresh lemon adds a natural essential oil, a strong aroma, and a zippy flavor to the salad, so I recommend it. No zester? A box grater will do just fine.

½ cup Dairy-Free Sour Cream (page 173) or store-bought dairy-free sour cream

3 tablespoons freshly squeezed lemon juice

2 tablespoons nutritional yeast

2 garlic cloves, minced

1 Medjool date, pitted (optional)

½ cup chopped walnuts

Grated zest of 1 lemon (optional)

2 large Honeycrisp or Gala apples, cored and cut into ¼-inch pieces

2 celery stalks, cut into ½-inch pieces

1 cup grapes (any kind), halved

1 head red-leaf lettuce, chopped or torn into bite-size pieces

1 head Bibb or Boston lettuce, chopped or torn into bite-size pieces

1. In a blender or food processor, combine the sour cream, lemon juice, nutritional yeast, garlic, and date (if using). Puree until creamy and pourable. Add 1 to 2 tablespoons of water, if needed, to make the dressing thinner. Set aside.

2. In a small bowl, stir together the walnuts and lemon zest (if using).

3. In a large bowl, combine the apples, celery, and grapes. Add the red-leaf and Bibb lettuces and toss to combine. Pour the dressing over the salad and toss until evenly coated.

4. Portion the salad into four bowls. Sprinkle 2 tablespoons of the walnut mixture over each salad and serve.

PER SERVING Calories: 265; Total Carbohydrates: 31g; Sugar: 21g; Total Fat: 16g; Saturated Fat: 6g; Sodium: 69mg; Protein: 6g; Fiber: 6g

Curried Lentil Soup with Cilantro Salsa

ALLERGEN-FREE **EGG-FREE** **GLUTEN-FREE** **NUT-FREE** **VEGAN**

SERVES 4

PREP TIME:
10 minutes

COOK TIME:
30 minutes

COOKING TIP: Use an immersion blender to avoid the risk of your blender exploding with hot soup.

This is my all-time favorite lentil soup. The soup is not at all traditional, but the flavors are so good I keep coming back to this version. The recipe is adapted from the vegan restaurant Vedge in Philadelphia. The soup served as one of my dietary staples when I was training for a half marathon over the winter. I came in from long runs with bright red cheeks and a deep hunger for its spicy, warming goodness.

1 small red onion, finely diced

1 cup minced fresh cilantro

2 scallions, white and green parts, trimmed and thinly sliced on a bias

1 teaspoon sea salt, plus more for seasoning

Juice of 1 lemon

1 tablespoon canola oil

1 yellow onion, minced

1 teaspoon minced peeled fresh ginger

1 tablespoon yellow curry powder

1 cup green lentils, picked over

8 cups vegetable broth

Freshly ground black pepper

1. In a large, lidded glass jar, combine the red onion, cilantro, scallions, salt, and lemon juice. Tightly seal the jar and shake to combine. Refrigerate for at least 30 minutes while the soup cooks.

2. In a large pot over medium heat, heat the oil. Add the yellow onion and ginger and cook for 5 minutes, stirring occasionally. Stir in the curry powder and cook for another minute.

3. Add the lentils and broth and bring the soup to a simmer. Cover the pot and simmer for 20 minutes. Transfer 2 cups of soup to a blender, vent the lid, and place a kitchen towel over it to protect from spattering (see Cooking Tip). Carefully puree until smooth. Return the pureed soup to the pot and season with salt and pepper.

4. Divide the soup among four serving bowls. Top with the red onion and cilantro salsa.

PER SERVING Calories: 303; Total Carbohydrates: 36g; Sugar: 5g; Total Fat: 7g; Saturated Fat: 1g; Sodium: 2,004mg; Protein: 23g; Fiber: 16g

Creamy Tortilla Soup

EGG-FREE GLUTEN-FREE MAKE ALLERGEN-FREE MAKE NUT-FREE

SERVES 4

PREP TIME:
10 minutes

COOK TIME:
25 minutes

SUBSTITUTION TIP: For a nut-free version, skip the cashew cream and stir in ½ cup Dairy-Free Sour Cream (page 173), or store-bought dairy-free sour cream.

If you're a soup enthusiast like me, you probably know how much fun it is to turn an everyday dinner item, such as tacos, into a comforting soup. Although I'm certainly not the first person to turn a meal into a soup, I did have to think outside the box a bit to make a satisfyingly rich and creamy dairy-free tortilla soup. I hope you'll love this version as much as I do.

1 tablespoon canola oil

1 red onion, diced

1 green bell pepper, diced

3 garlic cloves, minced

1 teaspoon ground cumin

1 teaspoon ground paprika

1 pound lean ground beef

Sea salt

Freshly ground black pepper

4 cups chicken broth

1 cup frozen corn, thawed

½ cup Cashew Cream (page 23)

2 tablespoons freshly squeezed lime juice

Lime wedges, for serving

4 cups blue corn tortilla chips, for serving

1. In a large pot over medium-high heat, heat the oil. Add the red onion and bell pepper and sauté for 3 to 4 minutes, until the vegetables begin to soften.

2. Stir in the garlic, cumin, and paprika. Cook for 1 minute.

3. Push the vegetables to the side of the pot and crumble the ground beef into the center. Season with salt and pepper. Cook for about 8 minutes, until lightly browned and just cooked through.

4. Add the broth to the pot, bring to a simmer, and cook for 5 minutes. Stir in the corn, cashew cream, and lime juice. Cook for 2 minutes more.

5. Serve the soup with the lime wedges and tortilla chips.

PER SERVING Calories: 431; Total Carbohydrates: 27g; Sugar: 4g; Total Fat: 20g; Saturated Fat: 6g; Sodium: 1,008mg; Protein: 32g; Fiber: 4g

Corn Chowder

EGG-FREE　**GLUTEN-FREE**　**NUT-FREE**　VEGAN

SERVES 4

PREP TIME:
10 minutes

COOK TIME:
35 minutes

SUBSTITUTION
TIP: To make
this soy-free,
substitute
½ cup nondairy
plain coffee
creamer, such
as So Deli-
cious Dairy
Free Original
Coconutmilk
Creamer, for
the sour cream.

Freshly shucked corn is a must in this dairy-free corn chowder that's perfect for late-summer lunches. The starch from the potato adds nice body and a creamy texture to the soup. The dairy-free sour cream infuses a bit of tang and even more creaminess for an absolutely decadent soup.

1 tablespoon canola oil

1 medium leek, trimmed, washed thoroughly, and diced

1 yellow onion, diced

Sea salt

1 russet potato, peeled and finely diced

4 thyme sprigs

4 cups vegetable broth

4 ears fresh corn, kernels removed, corncobs reserved

1 tablespoon white wine vinegar

½ cup Dairy-Free Sour Cream (page 173) or store-bought dairy-free sour cream

Freshly ground black pepper

2 scallions, green parts only, thinly sliced

1 tablespoon extra-virgin olive oil

Handful microgreens or sprouts, for garnish (optional)

1. In a medium pot over medium heat, heat the canola oil. Reduce the heat to low and add the leek, onion, and a generous pinch of salt to help the vegetables release their liquids. Cook for about 15 minutes, until soft and pulpy.

2. Add the potato, thyme, broth, and corncobs. Reserve ½ cup of the corn kernels for serving and add the remaining corn to the pot. Cook for 15 to 20 minutes.

3. Remove and discard the corncobs and thyme.

4. Stir in the vinegar, then add the sour cream.

5. Using an immersion blender, puree the soup until smooth. Season with salt and pepper.

6. Pour the soup into wide soup bowls. Garnish with the scallions, reserved corn kernels, olive oil, microgreens (if using), and a grind of pepper.

PER SERVING Calories: 352; Total Carbohydrates: 46g; Sugar: 10g; Total Fat: 16g; Saturated Fat: 7g; Sodium: 884mg; Protein: 12g; Fiber: 6g

Tom Yum Coconut Soup

EGG-FREE GLUTEN-FREE NUT-FREE

SERVES 4

PREP TIME:
10 minutes

COOK TIME:
20 minutes

INGREDIENT TIP: You can find tom yum paste in most larger grocery stores, or order it online. To make your own, use a mortar and pestle to mash 1 tablespoon minced lemongrass, 1 teaspoon minced galangal root, 4 shredded makrut lime leaves, and 2 Thai chiles.

My first taste of tom yum soup was at an authentic Thai restaurant and laundromat in north Portland. The spicy, tangy, and floral broth captivated me and I was eager to recreate it at home. Asian markets abound in Portland, so finding the lemongrass, makrut lime leaves, and galangal there was easy, but I know that isn't true of every town, so in this version, I call for tom yum paste. If you want to make your own, see the Ingredient Tip. This soup is delicious with steamed white rice and a simple side salad.

1 tablespoon canola oil

1 pound boneless, skinless chicken breast, cut into 2-inch pieces

1 onion, halved and thinly sliced

4 cups chicken broth

2 tablespoons tom yum paste

2 plum tomatoes, cored and diced

1 cup button mushrooms, quartered

1 teaspoon sugar

2 tablespoons fish sauce

3 tablespoons freshly squeezed lime juice

1 cup full-fat coconut milk

Sea salt

Freshly ground black pepper

1 cup roughly chopped fresh cilantro

2 scallions, white and green parts, trimmed and thinly sliced on a bias

1. In a large pot over medium-high heat, heat the oil. Add the chicken and onion and sauté for 10 minutes.

2. Stir in the broth, tom yum paste, tomatoes, and mushrooms. Cook for 5 minutes, until the chicken is cooked through and no longer pink and the vegetables are soft.

3. Stir in the sugar, fish sauce, lime juice, and coconut milk. Bring the soup to a simmer and cook for 1 minute. Season with salt and pepper.

4. Just before serving, stir in the cilantro and scallions.

PER SERVING Calories: 398; Total Carbohydrates: 13g; Sugar: 7g; Total Fat: 24g; Saturated Fat: 14g; Sodium: 1,980mg; Protein: 32g; Fiber: 3g

Creamy Tomato Soup

EGG-FREE **GLUTEN-FREE** MAKE VEGAN

SERVES 4

PREP TIME:
10 minutes

COOK TIME:
15 minutes

SUBSTITUTION
TIP: To make
this soup
vegan, use
vegetable broth
in place of the
chicken broth.

Tomato soup and grilled cheese sandwiches are a classic combo. This creamy tomato soup is thickened with cashew cream, and it pairs like a charm with a grilled cheese sandwich made with a dairy-free Cheddar cheese, such as Follow Your Heart.

2 tablespoons extra-virgin olive oil

3 garlic cloves, minced

2 shallots, thinly sliced

Pinch red pepper flakes

1 (28-ounce) can plum tomatoes, crushed, with juices

½ cup roughly chopped fresh basil, plus more for serving

2 cups chicken broth

½ cup Cashew Cream (page 23), plus 2 tablespoons

Sea salt

Freshly ground black pepper

1. In a large pot over medium-low heat, heat the oil. Stir in the garlic, shallots, red pepper flakes, tomatoes and their juices, and basil. Cook for 10 minutes, until soft and pulpy.

2. Pour in the broth and bring the soup to a gentle simmer. Cook for 5 minutes.

3. Remove the soup from the heat and let cool for 5 minutes. Puree the soup with an immersion blender. For a very smooth soup, pass it through a fine-mesh strainer as well.

4. Whisk in ½ cup of the cashew cream and season the soup with salt and pepper.

5. To serve, divide the soup among four serving bowls and swirl ½ tablespoon of the remaining cashew cream into each serving. Garnish each bowl with basil, as desired.

PER SERVING Calories: 192; Total Carbohydrates: 12g; Sugar: 7g; Total Fat: 15g; Saturated Fat: 8g; Sodium: 455mg; Protein: 5g; Fiber: 3g

Cream of Mushroom Soup

EGG-FREE   GLUTEN-FREE   MAKE ALLERGEN-FREE   MAKE VEGAN   NUT-FREE

SERVES 4

PREP TIME:
10 minutes

COOK TIME:
20 minutes

INGREDIENT TIP: For an even richer mushroom flavor, soak 1 ounce dried wild mushrooms in 1 cup boiling water for 10 minutes. Strain the mushrooms, reserving the liquid and discarding any sediment. Roughly chop the mushrooms and add them to the soup just before adding the sherry. Add the mushroom soaking liquid to the soup with 5 cups chicken broth instead of 6.

If you didn't think cream of mushroom soup was possible without cream, you're in for a surprise. Typically, I use cashew cream or dairy-free sour cream to thicken the soup and give it that creamy consistency, but this time I opted for white beans and dairy-free butter.

1 tablespoon canola oil

4 tablespoons (½ stick) dairy-free butter (such as Earth Balance Buttery Spread), divided

2 cups sliced mushrooms

1 small yellow onion, diced

2 garlic cloves, minced

1 teaspoon minced fresh thyme leaves

2 tablespoons sherry

6 cups chicken broth or vegetable broth

1 cup canned white beans (such as cannellini), drained and rinsed

Sea salt

Freshly ground black pepper

1. In a wide, deep skillet over medium-high heat, heat the oil and 1 tablespoon of the butter. Add a handful of mushrooms to the skillet and cook for 1 to 2 minutes per side. Push the cooked mushrooms to the side of the skillet and repeat until all the mushrooms are cooked.

2. Add the onion, garlic, and thyme to the skillet and cook for 5 minutes, stirring occasionally.

3. Pour the sherry into the skillet and cook for about 1 minute to cook off most of the alcohol. Add the broth, bring to a simmer, and cook for 1 minute.

4. Transfer 2 cups of the soup to a blender and add the white beans. Puree until very smooth. Return the pureed soup to the skillet and bring to a simmer for 1 minute.

5. Whisk in the remaining 3 tablespoons butter and season with salt and pepper.

PER SERVING Calories: 277; Total Carbohydrates: 17g; Sugar: 3g; Total Fat: 17g; Saturated Fat: 4g; Sodium: 1,424mg; Protein: 12g; Fiber: 6g

Snacks and Sides

Fruit and Nut Bars

EGG-FREE **GLUTEN-FREE** VEGAN

MAKES 8 BARS

PREP TIME:
10 minutes

This basic recipe can be taken in so many directions and is an essential part of my dairy-free snack repertoire. I love adding dairy-free dark chocolate chips and a splash of vanilla extract for a chocolate chip cookie dough version. Or I'll add cinnamon and orange zest for an autumn-spiced version.

FOR HEALTHY BROWNIE BARS

1¼ cups walnuts

Pinch sea salt

1 cup pitted dates

2 tablespoons unsweetened cocoa powder

½ teaspoon vanilla extract

FOR KEY LIME PIE BARS

¾ cup raw unsalted cashews

½ cup walnuts

Pinch sea salt

1 cup pitted dates

1 teaspoon grated lime zest

1 teaspoon freshly squeezed lime juice

FOR CHOCOLATE CHIP COOKIE DOUGH BARS

¾ cup walnuts

½ cup raw unsalted cashews

Pinch sea salt

1 cup pitted dates

½ cup dairy-free dark chocolate pieces

¼ teaspoon vanilla extract

FOR AUTUMN SPICE BARS

1¼ cups pecans

Pinch sea salt

1 cup pitted dates

1 teaspoon ground cinnamon

1 teaspoon grated orange zest

1 teaspoon freshly squeezed orange juice

TO MAKE THE BARS

1. In a food processor, combine the nuts and salt and pulse until coarsely ground.

2. Add the dates and process until fully blended.

3. Add the remaining variation add-ins and process just until integrated.

4. Spread the mixture on a clean cutting board. Press and form into a rectangle. Cut into 8 bars. Refrigerate in a covered container for up to 5 days.

HEALTHY BROWNIE BARS PER SERVING Calories: 99; Total Carbohydrates: 18g; Sugar: 14g; Total Fat: 3g; Saturated Fat: 0g; Sodium: 32mg; Protein: 1g; Fiber: 3g

KEY LIME PIE BARS PER SERVING Calories: 134; Total Carbohydrates: 20g; Sugar: 14g; Total Fat: 6g; Saturated Fat: 1g; Sodium: 33mg; Protein: 3g; Fiber: 2g

CHOCOLATE CHIP COOKIE DOUGH BARS PER SERVING Calories: 198; Total Carbohydrates: 29g; Sugar: 14g; Total Fat: 9g; Saturated Fat: 3g; Sodium: 32mg; Protein: 3g; Fiber: 2g

AUTUMN SPICE BARS PER SERVING Calories: 95; Total Carbohydrates: 18g; Sugar: 14g; Total Fat: 3g; Saturated Fat: 0g; Sodium: 32mg; Protein: 1g; Fiber: 2g

Marinated Chickpeas

ALLERGEN-FREE EGG-FREE GLUTEN-FREE NUT-FREE VEGAN

SERVES 4

PREP TIME:
10 minutes

COOKING TIP:
The flavors get even better as the chickpeas sit in the marinade, so if time allows, make this dish several hours in advance of when you intend to serve it.

Chickpeas are a good source of protein and complex carbohydrates and can be used in many different recipes—but they can be a little boring straight out of the can. This marinade transforms plain chickpeas into a delicious salad topping, side dish, or quick snack. The ingredient list is a bit long, but be assured, it is mostly pantry and grocery staples—such as oil, vinegar, and carrot—that you probably have on hand.

2 tablespoons red wine vinegar

1 tablespoon white wine vinegar

1 tablespoon extra-virgin olive oil

1 garlic clove, minced

1 teaspoon minced fresh thyme leaves, or ½ teaspoon dried

1 teaspoon grated lemon zest

1 carrot, minced

1 celery stalk, minced

1 shallot, minced

Sea salt

Freshly ground black pepper

2 (15-ounce) cans chickpeas, drained and rinsed

1. In a large, lidded jar, whisk the red wine vinegar, white wine vinegar, oil, garlic, thyme, lemon zest, carrot, celery, and shallot. Season generously with salt and pepper.

2. Add the chickpeas to the marinade, seal the jar tightly, and gently shake to combine.

3. Refrigerate, covered, for up to 4 days.

PER SERVING Calories: 329; Total Carbohydrates: 57g; Sugar: 1g; Total Fat: 6g; Saturated Fat: 1g; Sodium: 791mg; Protein: 12g; Fiber: 11g

Cranberry and Cracked Pepper Cheese Ball

EGG-FREE GLUTEN-FREE VEGAN

SERVES 6

PREP TIME:
5 minutes

**SERVING
TIP:** Serve
with sturdy
crackers or veg-
etable chips.

Your classic party appetizer is back! And this time it's dairy-free. Sweet, tart cranberries and savory shallot and thyme are the perfect complement to the Basic Nut Cheese.

1 recipe Basic Nut Cheese
   (page 28), made with cashews
   or macadamia nuts

2 tablespoons minced shallot

1 tablespoon minced
   fresh thyme leaves

Sea salt

Freshly ground black pepper

½ cup dried cranberries

1. Place the nut cheese into a nut milk bag or a colander lined with cheesecloth. Squeeze the excess moisture from the nut cheese with your hands, or set the colander over a bowl in the refrigerator and let it drain for 30 minutes, or until the nut cheese can hold its shape.

2. Place the nut cheese in a clean bowl. Stir in the shallot and thyme. Season with salt and pepper. Form the cheese into a small ball.

3. On a small plate, spread out the dried cranberries, then roll the cheese ball in the cranberries until the ball is covered. Transfer to a serving platter, or cover and refrigerate until ready to serve.

PER SERVING Calories: 117; Total Carbohydrates: 8g; Sugar: 3g; Total Fat: 8g; Saturated Fat: 1g; Sodium: 66mg; Protein: 3g; Fiber: 1g

Pistachio and Herb "Goat" Cheese

EGG-FREE GLUTEN-FREE VEGAN

SERVES 6

PREP TIME:
5 minutes

SERVING TIP:
Serve this
cheese with
oil-packed
sundried
tomatoes and
crostini for
a decadent
appetizer.

Grassy herbs and sweet, salty pistachios form a delicious crust around Basic Nut Cheese. A variety of herbs will work in this recipe, so use what you have. I like fresh tarragon, cilantro, and oregano as well as the trio called for here.

1 recipe Basic Nut Cheese (page 28), made with cashews or macadamia nuts

1 tablespoon minced fresh thyme leaves

1 tablespoon minced fresh basil

1 tablespoon minced fresh parsley

¼ cup finely chopped pistachios

1. Place the nut cheese into a nut milk bag or a colander lined with cheesecloth. Squeeze the excess moisture from the nut cheese with your hands, or set the colander over a bowl in the refrigerator and let it drain for 30 minutes, or until the nut cheese can hold its shape.

2. On a small plate, stir together the thyme, basil, parsley, and pistachios and spread the mixture over the plate.

3. Form the cheese into a small log, then roll it in the herb and nut mixture. Transfer to a serving platter, or cover and refrigerate until ready to serve.

PER SERVING Calories: 119; Total Carbohydrates: 6g; Sugar: 0g; Total Fat: 9g; Saturated Fat: 1g; Sodium: 84mg; Protein: 4g; Fiber: 1g

Sweet Potato Hummus

ALLERGEN-FREE **EGG-FREE** **GLUTEN-FREE** **NUT-FREE** **VEGAN**

SERVES 8

PREP TIME:
5 minutes

COOK TIME:
50 minutes

COOKING TIP:
Spread a layer of aluminum foil on the oven rack beneath the sweet potato to catch any sugary drips.

Let me say first, this sweet potato hummus is nothing like traditional hummus and is only so named because it contains chickpeas. However, the dip is savory and delicious, and works nicely as a dip for chips or vegetables or in Sweet Potato Quesadillas (page 138).

1 medium sweet potato, scrubbed

1 (15-ounce) can chickpeas, drained and rinsed

1 canned chipotle pepper in adobo, minced, plus 1 teaspoon adobo sauce from the can

2 tablespoons nutritional yeast

2 teaspoons apple cider vinegar

1 teaspoon sugar

½ teaspoon sea salt

1. Preheat the oven to 400°F.

2. Prick the sweet potato all over with a fork and bake for 50 minutes, or until the sweet potato is very tender and syrup oozes from the holes in the skin.

3. Carefully scrape the roasted sweet potato flesh into a blender. Add the chickpeas, chipotle, adobo sauce, nutritional yeast, vinegar, sugar, and salt. Puree until smooth, stopping to scrape down the sides of the blender as needed.

PER SERVING Calories: 94; Total Carbohydrates: 18g; Sugar: 1g; Total Fat: 1g; Saturated Fat: 0g; Sodium: 302mg; Protein: 4g; Fiber: 4g

Spinach-Artichoke Dip

EGG-FREE **GLUTEN-FREE** **VEGAN**

SERVES 6

PREP TIME:
15 minutes,
plus at least
30 minutes
to soak

COOK TIME:
30 minutes

**INGREDIENT
TIP:** Silken tofu
is available in
most grocery
stores and is
not typically
refrigerated.
Regular soft
tofu can be
used in a pinch,
but it lacks the
creamy texture
of silken tofu.

SERVING TIP:
Serve with
sliced vegeta-
bles or chips.

Soaked cashews and creamy silken tofu come together to create a luxurious sauce in this classic chip-dip stand-in.

1 tablespoon canola oil

1 yellow onion, diced

4 garlic cloves, minced

1 teaspoon minced fresh thyme leaves or ½ teaspoon dried

Pinch red pepper flakes

2 tablespoons freshly squeezed lemon juice

1 (12-ounce) package silken tofu

½ cup raw unsalted cashews, soaked in cold water for 8 hours or hot water for 30 minutes, drained, and rinsed

1 teaspoon garlic powder

½ teaspoon sea salt

¼ to ½ cup water

2 cups roughly chopped fresh spinach

1 (15-ounce) can artichoke hearts, drained and quartered

2 tablespoons Plant-Based Parmesan (page 27; optional)

1. Preheat the oven to 350°F.

2. In a large oven-safe skillet over medium heat, warm the oil. Add the onion, garlic, thyme, and red pepper flakes and cook for 5 to 7 minutes.

3. Meanwhile, in a blender, combine the lemon juice, tofu, cashews, garlic powder, and salt. Puree until very smooth, adding only as much water as needed to keep the blender moving. Set aside.

4. Add the spinach to the skillet and cook for about 3 minutes, until thoroughly wilted and the moisture has evaporated.

5. Add the artichoke hearts and cook until just heated through.

6. Pour the cashew and tofu mixture into the skillet, stir, then smooth into an even layer. Top with the Parmesan (if using).

7. Bake, uncovered, for 15 to 20 minutes, until the top forms a light crust.

PER SERVING Calories: 157; Total Carbohydrates: 15g; Sugar: 3g; Total Fat: 8g; Saturated Fat: 1g; Sodium: 254mg; Protein: 9g; Fiber: 5g

Polenta Fries

ALLERGEN-FREE   EGG-FREE   GLUTEN-FREE   NUT-FREE   VEGAN

SERVES 4

PREP TIME:
10 minutes

COOK TIME:
45 minutes

Creamy polenta is traditionally made with milk and Parmesan. But for these oven fries, the packaged polenta, which is typically dairy-free, is also hassle-free. Even better, the prepared polenta is super easy to slice into fries that are perfect for dipping in savory Pomodoro Sauce.

1 (18-ounce) package prepared dairy-free polenta

2 tablespoons extra-virgin olive oil

1 tablespoon minced fresh rosemary leaves (optional)

Sea salt

Freshly ground black pepper

1 cup Pomodoro Sauce (page 177) or good-quality store-bought marinara sauce, warmed

1. Preheat the oven to 425°F. Line a sheet pan with parchment paper.

2. Halve the polenta crosswise, then cut it into ½- to 1-inch-thick spears. Carefully place the polenta spears on the prepared pan and drizzle with oil. Season with rosemary (if using), salt, and pepper. Turn the spears to coat in the oil.

3. Bake for 40 to 45 minutes, until golden and crisp on the outside. Serve with the warmed sauce for dipping.

PER SERVING Calories: 204; Total Carbohydrates: 28g; Sugar: 7g; Total Fat: 9g; Saturated Fat: 1g; Sodium: 710mg; Protein: 4g; Fiber: 3g

Nacho Cheese Dip

EGG-FREE MAKE GLUTEN-FREE VEGAN

SERVES 6

PREP TIME:
15 minutes,
plus at least
30 minutes
to soak

COOK TIME:
30 minutes

**INGREDIENT
TIP:** Chipotle
peppers in
adobo sauce
can be found in
most grocery
stores. Wheat
is sometimes
added as a
thickener, so
read the labels
carefully if you
follow a gluten-
free diet.

This dip is spicy, smoky, and creamy. Like the Spinach-Artichoke Dip (page 71), this creamy base is made with cashews and silken tofu. It gets a boost of color and flavor from steamed carrot and cheesy flavor from nutritional yeast.

1 cup diced carrots

1 tablespoon canola oil

1 yellow onion, diced

2 garlic cloves, minced

½ cup raw unsalted cashews, soaked in cold water for 8 hours or hot water for 30 minutes, drained, and rinsed

1 (12-ounce) package silken tofu

2 tablespoons nutritional yeast

2 tablespoons freshly squeezed lime juice

1 tablespoon tomato paste

1 to 2 teaspoons minced canned chipotle pepper in adobo

1 teaspoon smoked paprika

1 teaspoon garlic powder

½ teaspoon ground cumin

½ teaspoon sea salt

¼ to ½ cup water

Corn tortilla chips, for serving

1. Preheat the oven to 350°F.

2. In a steamer basket set over simmering water, steam the carrots for 5 to 7 minutes, until tender. Transfer the carrots to a blender.

3. While the carrots cook, in a large oven-safe skillet over medium heat, heat the oil. Add the onion and garlic and cook for 3 to 4 minutes, until the vegetables begin to soften.

4. In a blender, combine the cashews, tofu, nutritional yeast, lime juice, tomato paste, chipotle, paprika, garlic powder, cumin, and salt. Blend, adding only as much water as needed to keep the blender moving.

5. Pour the cashew and tofu mixture into the skillet, give everything a good stir, then smooth into an even layer.

6. Bake, uncovered, for 15 to 20 minutes, until the top forms a light crust.

7. Serve with the tortilla chips.

PER SERVING Calories: 141; Total Carbohydrates: 10g; Sugar: 3g; Total Fat: 8g; Saturated Fat: 1g; Sodium: 195mg; Protein: 8g; Fiber: 2g

Spicy Jalapeño Baked Taquitos

EGG-FREE **GLUTEN-FREE** **MAKE ALLERGEN-FREE** **MAKE VEGAN** **NUT-FREE**

SERVES 4

PREP TIME:
10 minutes

COOK TIME:
15 minutes

INGREDIENT TIP: If you want to keep these vegan and allergen-free, read the label of the refried beans to ensure they don't contain lard or allergens such as soy.

I cannot express the level of disappointment I felt when I discovered that the Trader Joe's black bean taquitos I had just bitten into had cheese in them. They were perfectly crisp on the outside, and savory and spicy on the inside. I needed to create a dairy-free alternative! Though you certainly could make the refried beans from scratch with fresh onion, jalapeño, and spices, I wanted a recipe that was almost as easy as store-bought. The kids love these taquitos for snack time, and they're healthier than the original.

12 (6-inch) corn tortillas

1 (15-ounce) can spicy jalapeño or salsa-style vegetarian refried black beans

2 tablespoons canola oil

1 cup prepared guacamole, for serving

1. Preheat the oven to 425°F.

2. Heat the corn tortillas individually in the microwave for about 10 seconds each to soften and place on a work surface.

3. Place 2 generous tablespoons of the refried beans in a line down one side of each tortilla, about one-third of the way in from the edge, and roll the tortillas into tight cylinders. Place the rolled tortillas on a sheet pan, seam-side down. Lightly brush the tortillas with oil.

4. Bake for 15 minutes, or until the tortillas are crisp and beginning to brown. Let cool for a few minutes before serving with the guacamole on the side.

PER SERVING Calories: 440; Total Carbohydrates: 49g; Sugar: 3g; Total Fat: 26g; Saturated Fat: 3g; Sodium: 464mg; Protein: 9g; Fiber: 12g

Sweet Potato Corn Cakes

MAKE GLUTEN-FREE **NUT-FREE** **VEGETARIAN**

SERVES 4

PREP TIME:
5 minutes

COOK TIME:
30 minutes

**VARIATION
TIP:** You can
make these
cakes with any
starchy root
vegetable, such
as potatoes,
parsnips, or
turnips.

These delicious sweet potato cakes fall somewhere between latkes and
corn fritters. Their flavor is spicy and savory and the cakes are perfectly
crisp on the outside. They pair well with Turkey Mushroom Stew
(page 131).

2 medium sweet
   potatoes, grated

1 cup corn kernels

1 teaspoon smoked paprika

½ teaspoon ground cumin

¼ cup all-purpose flour or
   gluten-free flour blend

½ teaspoon sea salt

1 large egg, whisked

1. Preheat the oven to 400°F. Line a sheet pan with parchment paper.

2. In a small bowl, stir together the sweet potatoes, corn, paprika,
   cumin, flour, salt, and egg. Form the mixture into 8 small patties and
   place them on the prepared sheet pan.

3. Bake for 25 to 30 minutes, until the cakes are crisp on the outside and
   tender on the inside.

PER SERVING Calories: 168; Total Carbohydrates: 35g; Sugar: 2g; Total Fat: 2g;
Saturated Fat: 1g; Sodium: 262mg; Protein: 5g; Fiber: 5g

Vegetable Bake with Cayenne Pepper

ALLERGEN-FREE EGG-FREE GLUTEN-FREE NUT-FREE VEGAN

SERVES 12

PREP TIME:
20 minutes

COOK TIME:
1 hour

SUBSTITUTION TIP: Make this dish your own by substituting different vegetables. Broccoli, cauliflower, or asparagus could all take the place of the Brussels sprouts—or just add them to the mix. You may need to adjust the cooking time a bit when using more delicate vegetables.

Making a big pan of roasted vegetables at the beginning of the week sets you up with side dishes for grilled meats or toppings for fried eggs for a quick breakfast-for-dinner option. Brussels sprouts are excellent for this kind of dish because they're sturdy enough to hold up during the long bake without turning mushy. The sprouts' leafy edges tend to brown and crisp, giving the dish delicious texture.

1 pound Brussels sprouts (about 20), trimmed and halved

1 tomato, roughly chopped

1 bunch radishes (about 12), trimmed and quartered

1 onion, cut into 1-inch pieces

2 turnips, trimmed and quartered

6 tablespoons olive oil

¼ cup cayenne pepper

2 teaspoons salt

1 teaspoon freshly ground black pepper

1. Preheat the oven to 400°F.

2. On a large sheet pan, toss together the Brussels sprouts, tomato, radishes, onion, and turnips. Drizzle with the oil and toss to coat well. Season with cayenne, salt, and pepper.

3. Bake for 1 hour, or until the vegetables are browned and crisp.

4. Refrigerate leftovers, covered, for up to 1 week.

PER SERVING Calories: 91; Total Carbohydrates: 7g; Sugar: 2g; Total Fat: 7g; Saturated Fat: 1g; Sodium: 412mg; Protein: 2g; Fiber: 2g

Creamy Miso Shiitake Kale

EGG-FREE NUT-FREE VEGAN

SERVES 4

PREP TIME:
5 minutes, plus
10 minutes
to soak

COOK TIME:
30 minutes

This side dish combines the umami, or savory, flavors of miso and mushrooms in a thick coconut cream sauce. The garlic nicely masks any coconut undertones, so no one will ever know it's dairy-free! If you don't have dried shiitake mushrooms, use another dried wild mushroom. If you prefer fresh mushrooms, slice them and cook in step 2 with the shallot and garlic. Use 1 cup vegetable broth in place of the mushroom soaking liquid.

½ ounce dried shiitake mushrooms

1 cup hot water

1 tablespoon canola oil or extra-virgin olive oil

1 shallot, thinly sliced

3 garlic cloves, minced

Sea salt

2 bunches kale, leaves roughly chopped, stems minced

½ cup full-fat coconut milk

1 tablespoon white miso paste

½ teaspoon low-sodium soy sauce

¾ teaspoon red wine vinegar

Freshly ground black pepper

1. In a small bowl, cover the mushrooms with the hot water and set aside for 10 minutes to soak.

2. In a large skillet over medium heat, heat the oil. Add the shallot, garlic, and a pinch of salt. Cook for 3 to 4 minutes, until softened.

3. With a slotted spoon, strain the mushrooms, reserving the soaking liquid. Strain the soaking liquid to remove any sediment.

4. Roughly chop the mushrooms. Add them to the skillet, along with their soaking liquid and the kale. Bring to a simmer and cook for about 20 minutes, until the kale is very soft and the liquid has mostly evaporated.

5. Stir in the coconut milk, miso, soy sauce, and vinegar. Cook for 1 to 2 minutes to allow the flavors to come together and the sauce to thicken slightly. Season with salt and pepper and serve.

PER SERVING Calories: 207; Total Carbohydrates: 23g; Sugar: 1g; Total Fat: 11g; Saturated Fat: 7g; Sodium: 333mg; Protein: 7g; Fiber: 5g

Scalloped Potatoes

EGG-FREE **MAKE GLUTEN-FREE** **VEGAN**

SERVES 6

PREP TIME:
10 minutes

COOK TIME:
40 minutes

INGREDIENT TIP: I like to use starchy potatoes, such as russets, in this recipe because their starch thickens the sauce as they cook.

Creamy on the inside with a nice golden crust on the outside, these scalloped potatoes are comfort food to the max. Perfect for holiday gatherings or summer barbecues, this dish will win over even the toughest critic.

3 tablespoons dairy-free butter (such as Earth Balance Buttery Spread), divided

2 tablespoons all-purpose flour or gluten-free flour blend

2 cups vegetable broth

1 teaspoon minced garlic

1 teaspoon minced fresh thyme leaves

1 teaspoon sea salt

1½ cups Cashew Cream (page 23)

2 pounds baking potatoes, sliced paper-thin

¼ cup Plant-Based Parmesan (page 27; optional)

1. Preheat the oven to 375°F. Coat the interior of a 2-quart casserole dish with 1 tablespoon of the butter.

2. In a medium saucepan over medium heat, melt the remaining 2 tablespoons butter. Add the flour and cook for about 1 minute, whisking until thick and bubbling. Pour in the broth and whisk constantly until thickened.

3. Stir in the garlic, thyme, salt, and cashew cream.

4. Spread the potatoes in the prepared casserole dish and pour the sauce over the top, stirring just to distribute the sauce. Top with the Parmesan (if using).

5. Bake, uncovered, for 40 minutes, until the potatoes are tender and the top is browned and bubbling.

PER SERVING Calories: 270; Total Carbohydrates: 29g; Sugar: 3g; Total Fat: 16g; Saturated Fat: 10g; Sodium: 637mg; Protein: 5g; Fiber: 5g

Mashed Potatoes

EGG-FREE GLUTEN-FREE VEGAN

SERVES 4

PREP TIME:
5 minutes

COOK TIME:
15 minutes

COOKING TIP:
If you use a
potato ricer,
you do not
need to peel
the potatoes.

I love the texture and flavor of mashed potatoes with dairy-free sour cream. If you prefer to skip that step, simply use another ½ to 1 cup almond milk.

2½ pounds Yukon Gold
potatoes, peeled
and quartered

Sea salt

1 cup Dairy-Free Sour Cream
(page 173) or store-bought
dairy-free sour cream

2 tablespoons dairy-free
butter (such as Earth
Balance Buttery Spread)

½ to 1 cup Plain Nut Milk
(page 22), made with almonds

2 tablespoons minced fresh
chives, for garnish (optional)

1. Put the potatoes in a large pot of salted water. Bring to a boil and cook for about 15 minutes, until the potatoes are fork-tender. Drain the potatoes thoroughly and return them to the pot.

2. Stir in the sour cream and butter, then mash with a potato masher. While mashing, add enough almond milk to thin the potatoes to your desired consistency.

3. Serve garnished with chives (if using).

PER SERVING Calories: 373; Total Carbohydrates: 49g; Sugar: 7g; Total Fat: 18g; Saturated Fat: 12g; Sodium: 226mg; Protein: 6g; Fiber: 7g

Bourbon Mashed Sweet Potatoes

EGG-FREE **GLUTEN-FREE** **MAKE ALLERGEN-FREE** **MAKE NUT-FREE** **VEGAN**

SERVES 6

PREP TIME:
10 minutes

COOK TIME:
45 minutes

SUBSTITUTION TIP: To make this dish nut-free, omit the pecans.

I tried these sweet potatoes for the first time at Thanksgiving and wanted to skip dessert just so I could lick the casserole dish clean. They're that good!—and much healthier than the traditional marshmallow-topped sweet potatoes that are ubiquitous around the holidays.

8 tablespoons (1 stick) dairy-free butter (such as Earth Balance Buttery Spread), plus 1 tablespoon

2 pounds sweet potatoes, peeled and cut into 1-inch pieces

¼ cup bourbon

¼ cup packed brown sugar

½ teaspoon sea salt

1 cup pecan halves, toasted

1. Preheat the oven to 375°F. Coat the interior of a 2-quart casserole dish with 1 tablespoon of the butter.

2. In a steamer over simmering water, steam the sweet potatoes for 20 minutes, or until tender. Drain and transfer the sweet potatoes to a large bowl.

3. Add the bourbon, brown sugar, the remaining 8 tablespoons (1 stick) butter, and the salt. With a potato masher, mash until smooth. Spread the mixture into the casserole dish, and top with the pecans.

4. Bake, uncovered, for 25 minutes, until the pecans are lightly browned and the potatoes are mostly set in the center.

PER SERVING Calories: 499; Total Carbohydrates: 51g; Sugar: 7g; Total Fat: 30g; Saturated Fat: 6g; Sodium: 336mg; Protein: 4g; Fiber: 8g

Fish and Seafood

Clam Chowder

EGG-FREE **GLUTEN-FREE** **MAKE NUT-FREE**

SERVES 4

PREP TIME:
10 minutes

COOK TIME:
45 minutes

**SUBSTITUTION
TIP:** To make
this soup
without bacon,
cook the
vegetables in
2 tablespoons
dairy-free
butter.
Add ¼ to
½ teaspoon
liquid smoke
when you add
the clams.

Growing up in the Pacific Northwest, I knew that seafood was always on the menu, and I learned to like it from a young age, especially clam chowder. On dark days, a steaming bowl of chowder was the perfect antidote to a rained-out camping trip in the San Juan Islands or a drizzly hike through the Columbia Gorge.

4 bacon slices, roughly chopped

4 celery stalks, finely diced

1 onion, finely diced

4 garlic cloves, minced

Sea salt

1 cup clam juice

1 thyme sprig

4 medium potatoes, peeled and diced

4 cups Plain Nut Milk (page 22), made with almonds, or Soy Milk (page 24), divided

2 (6-ounce) cans clams, drained and roughly chopped

Freshly ground black pepper

1. In a large pot over medium-low heat, cook the bacon for 10 minutes, until it has rendered most of its fat. Transfer the bacon to a dish, leaving the fat in the pot.

2. Add the celery, onion, and garlic to the pot and season with salt. Cook for 10 minutes.

3. Pour in the clam juice, add the thyme, and bring to a simmer.

4. Add the potatoes, cover the pot, and cook for 25 minutes, until tender. Remove and discard the thyme. Transfer about 1 cup of the potatoes to a blender, add 1 cup of the nut milk, and puree until smooth. Return the puree to the pot and add the remaining 3 cups nut milk.

5. Bring the chowder to a gentle simmer, stir in the clams and bacon, and cook just until heated through.

6. Season with salt and pepper before serving.

PER SERVING Calories: 318; Total Carbohydrates: 40g; Sugar: 4g; Total Fat: 12g; Saturated Fat: 3g; Sodium: 885mg; Protein: 14g; Fiber: 7g

Shrimp Bisque

EGG-FREE   MAKE GLUTEN-FREE   MAKE NUT-FREE

SERVES 4

PREP TIME:
15 minutes

COOK TIME:
40 minutes

INGREDIENT TIP: If you follow a nut-free diet, choose a dairy-free cream that doesn't contain nuts. The brand suggested in this recipe contains almond milk and coconut cream.

This creamy seafood soup is sweet and savory, with just the right amount of kick from cayenne pepper. You can make it ahead but wait to cook the shrimp and stir in the dairy-free cream until right before serving. My favorite gluten-free flour blend for thickening soups and sauces is Bob's Red Mill Gluten Free 1-to-1 Baking Flour.

1½ pounds large shrimp

6 cups water

Sea salt

1 leek, trimmed, halved, and thoroughly cleaned

2 garlic cloves, smashed

2 celery stalks, roughly chopped

2 carrots, roughly chopped

4 tablespoons (½ stick) dairy-free butter (such as Earth Balance Buttery Spread)

¼ cup all-purpose flour or gluten-free flour blend

Grated zest of 1 orange

2 tablespoons tomato paste

½ teaspoon cayenne pepper

1 cup dairy-free cream (such as Califia Dairy Free Better Half)

Freshly ground black pepper

1. Peel the shrimp and place the peels in a large pot over medium heat. Cover with the water, add a pinch of salt, the leek, garlic, celery, and carrots. Bring to a simmer and cook for 20 minutes. Strain the broth, reserving it, discarding the shells and vegetables. Set the broth aside.

2. Wipe the pot clean, then return it to medium heat. Combine the butter and flour in the pot and cook for 1 to 2 minutes, whisking constantly until thick and bubbling.

3. Pour in the shrimp broth, whisking vigorously. Add the orange zest, tomato paste, and cayenne. Simmer for 5 minutes to thicken.

4. Add the shrimp and simmer for 2 to 3 minutes, until cooked through. Stir in the cream and cook until just heated through. Season with salt and pepper.

PER SERVING Calories: 469; Total Carbohydrates: 35g; Sugar: 23g; Total Fat: 19g; Saturated Fat: 9g; Sodium: 604mg; Protein: 38g; Fiber: 2g

Butternut Squash and Shrimp Curry

EGG-FREE GLUTEN-FREE NUT-FREE

SERVES 4

PREP TIME:
10 minutes

COOK TIME:
25 minutes

INGREDIENT TIP: To process the butternut squash, remove all of the peel with a vegetable peeler. Halve the squash lengthwise and scoop out the seeds with a spoon. Cut the squash into 1-inch spears, then cut the spears into 1-inch dice.

This Thai-inspired curry bowl is brimming with Southeast Asian flavors. Creamy coconut milk, pungent fish sauce, and fragrant lemongrass combine for an unforgettably addicting broth. The butternut squash provides some carbs, but for an even more filling meal, serve with rice.

1 tablespoon coconut oil

1 red onion, halved and sliced

4 garlic cloves, minced

1 (1-inch) piece fresh ginger, peeled and minced

1 Thai chile, minced

1 tablespoon minced lemongrass

1 tablespoon fish sauce

1 (15-ounce) can coconut milk

4 cups diced butternut squash (see Ingredient Tip)

1½ pounds shrimp, peeled and deveined

1 tablespoon freshly squeezed lime juice

Sea salt

Freshly ground black pepper

½ cup fresh cilantro leaves

1. In a large pot over medium heat, heat the oil. Add the onion, garlic, ginger, and chile. Cook for about 5 minutes, stirring occasionally, until fragrant and nearly soft.

2. Add the lemongrass, fish sauce, and coconut milk. Bring to a simmer and add the butternut squash. Cover the pot and simmer for about 15 minutes, until the butternut squash is tender.

3. Add the shrimp to the soup and simmer for 2 to 3 minutes, or until the shrimp are cooked through.

4. Stir in the lime juice and season the soup with salt and pepper.

5. Sprinkle with the cilantro before serving.

PER SERVING Calories: 530; Total Carbohydrates: 28g; Sugar: 9g; Total Fat: 31g; Saturated Fat: 26g; Sodium: 811mg; Protein: 40g; Fiber: 6g

Cod with Tomato-Basil Sauce

EGG-FREE GLUTEN-FREE NUT-FREE

SERVES 4

PREP TIME:
10 minutes

COOK TIME:
25 minutes

**VARIATION
TIP:** For more
Mediterranean
flavors, use
halibut and add
1 tablespoon
minced fresh
oregano
leaves and
½ cup whole
green olives
to the skillet.

This easy one-pan supper has become one of my favorite recipes for using cod, which can sometimes taste a little fishy. The spicy red pepper flakes, tangy tomatoes, lemon, and sweet basil are an addicting combination and pack a nice flavor punch for minimal effort. This dish is especially great in late summer, when tomatoes and basil are at their peak.

2 tablespoons
  extra-virgin olive oil

2 teaspoons minced garlic

Pinch red pepper flakes

2 pints grape tomatoes, halved

½ cup dry white wine

2 tablespoons freshly
  squeezed lemon juice

½ cup roughly chopped
  fresh basil, divided

4 (4- to 6-ounce) cod fillets

Sea salt

Freshly ground black pepper

1. In a large skillet over medium heat, heat the oil. Add the garlic and red pepper flakes and cook for 30 seconds until fragrant.

2. Add the tomatoes and cook for about 10 minutes, until thoroughly broken down.

3. Add the wine and cook for 2 to 3 minute to burn off some of the alcohol. Add the lemon juice and ¼ cup of the basil.

4. Season the cod fillets with salt and pepper. Place them in the skillet and spoon some of the tomato-basil mixture on top. Simmer for 3 to 4 minutes, flip, and cook for 3 to 4 minutes more, or until the fish flakes easily with a fork.

5. Garnish with the remaining ¼ cup basil just before serving.

PER SERVING Calories: 258; Total Carbohydrates: 9g; Sugar: 5g; Total Fat: 9g; Saturated Fat: 1g; Sodium: 192mg; Protein: 32g; Fiber: 2g

Miso-Glazed Cod

SERVES 4

PREP TIME:
5 minutes

COOK TIME:
20 minutes

INGREDIENT TIP: Miso is fermented soybean paste with a salty, sweet, complex flavor. Choose mellow white miso for this recipe.

SUBSTITUTION TIP: To make this dish gluten-free, use gluten-free soy sauce.

This Japanese-inspired baked cod is a bit sweet from honey, with unexpected flavors that come from the mellow white miso paste. Double the sauce to add to some sautéed vegetables. Serve with steamed rice or buckwheat noodles.

2 tablespoons white miso paste

2 tablespoons low-sodium soy sauce

1 tablespoon rice vinegar

1 tablespoon toasted sesame oil

1½ teaspoons honey

4 (4- to 6-ounce) cod fillets

2 tablespoons sesame seeds

1. Preheat the oven to 350°F.

2. In a small bowl, whisk the miso, soy sauce, vinegar, oil, and honey to blend.

3. Place the cod in a baking dish and cover with the miso sauce, turning the fish to coat.

4. Cover the dish and bake for 10 minutes. Remove the cover and bake for 5 to 10 minutes more, or until the cod is cooked through and flakes easily with a fork.

5. Meanwhile, toast the sesame seeds in a dry skillet over medium heat for about 3 minutes, until golden brown and fragrant. Sprinkle the toasted sesame seeds over the cod to serve.

PER SERVING Calories: 220; Total Carbohydrates: 7g; Sugar: 3g; Total Fat: 7g; Saturated Fat: 1g; Sodium: 832mg; Protein: 32g; Fiber: 1g

Sole Meunière

EGG-FREE   MAKE GLUTEN-FREE   NUT-FREE

SERVES 2

PREP TIME:
5 minutes

COOK TIME:
5 minutes

SUBSTITUTION TIP: Sole is not always a sustainable seafood option, so you can use another flaky, flat white fish if you like.

I first enjoyed sole meunière in England after purchasing fresh fish in Aldeburgh, a small town on the North Sea. I was thrilled to discover that the classic French recipe—a highlight of Julia Child's early dining experiences in France—is a cinch to prepare. It is traditionally made with browned butter, however, the Maillard reaction also occurs using dairy-free butter, yielding that delicious, browned taste.

¼ cup all-purpose flour or gluten-free flour blend

½ teaspoon fine sea salt

¼ teaspoon freshly ground black pepper

2 (10- to 14-ounce) whole sole fillets

2 tablespoons dairy-free butter (such as Earth Balance Buttery Spread)

Juice of 1 lemon

1 tablespoon minced fresh parsley

1. In a shallow dish, mix together the flour, salt, and pepper. Pat the fish dry with paper towels and dredge it in the flour mixture.

2. In a wide skillet over medium-high heat, melt the butter. Sear the fish on one side for about 2 minutes. Carefully turn the fish and cook on the other side for 1 to 2 minutes, or until just cooked through. Transfer the fish to a serving platter.

3. Drizzle the lemon juice into the skillet, scraping up the browned bits with a wooden spoon, then pour the sauce over the cooked fish and sprinkle the fish with parsley. Serve immediately.

PER SERVING Calories: 508; Total Carbohydrates: 12g; Sugar: 0g; Total Fat: 18g; Saturated Fat: 3g; Sodium: 894mg; Protein: 75g; Fiber: 1g

Cajun Blackened Halibut with Sautéed Peppers

EGG-FREE GLUTEN-FREE NUT-FREE

SERVES 4

PREP TIME:
10 minutes

COOK TIME:
15 minutes

COOKING TIP:
For extra flavor, coat the fish in the spice paste up to 8 hours ahead and keep refrigerated until ready to cook.

Here, spicy blackened halibut joins sautéed peppers and onions in a tangy pan sauce. Although blackening might suggest the fish is burned, it is not. Blackening spices darken when cooked, but the fish remains perfectly moist. Serve this tasty dish with steamed rice.

2 tablespoons Cajun blackening spice

2 tablespoons minced fresh parsley

1 teaspoon minced fresh garlic

3 tablespoons canola oil, divided

½ teaspoon sea salt, plus more for seasoning

¼ teaspoon freshly ground black pepper, plus more for seasoning

4 (4- to 6-ounce) halibut fillets

1 red or yellow bell pepper, cored and thinly sliced

1 green bell pepper, cored and thinly sliced

½ yellow onion, thinly sliced

¼ cup white wine

1 tablespoon freshly squeezed lemon juice

1. With a mortar and pestle, crush the blackening spice, parsley, garlic, 2 tablespoons of the oil, the salt, and pepper until it forms a paste. Spread the paste onto the fish, coating all sides.

2. Heat a large skillet over medium-high heat. Place the fillets in the hot skillet and cook for 3 to 4 minutes per side until they are dark on the outside and flake easily with a fork. Transfer to a serving platter.

3. Pour the remaining 1 tablespoon oil into the skillet. Add the red and green bell peppers and onion and sauté for about 3 minutes just until softened and beginning to brown.

4. Add the wine and lemon juice and cook for 2 minutes. Season with salt and pepper. Serve the vegetables alongside the fish.

PER SERVING Calories: 303; Total Carbohydrates: 6g; Sugar: 3g; Total Fat: 15g; Saturated Fat: 1g; Sodium: 349mg; Protein: 36g; Fiber: 1g

Spicy Italian Sausage and Mussels over Fettucine

EGG-FREE NUT-FREE

SERVES 4

PREP TIME:
15 minutes

COOK TIME:
30 minutes

INGREDIENT TIP: If you want a little more spice than the Italian sausage brings to the party, add a generous pinch of red pepper flakes.

Is there anything more comforting than a giant shared platter of pasta topped with flavorful sausage, tomatoes, and fresh mussels? It's one of my favorite dishes to serve company because we can enjoy it family style, and dinner lasts a little longer because the mussels are still in their shells.

Sea salt

12 ounces fettucine

2 tablespoons olive oil

1 red onion, halved and thinly sliced

6 garlic cloves, smashed

2 links spicy Italian sausage, casings removed

1 cup dry white wine

½ cup chicken broth

2 tablespoons tomato paste

1 (15-ounce) can whole plum tomatoes, drained and crushed

½ cup hand-torn fresh basil leaves

2 pounds fresh mussels, scrubbed and debearded

1. Bring a large pot of salted water to a boil and cook the pasta according to the package directions. Drain the pasta and set aside.

2. While the pasta cooks, in another large pot over medium heat, heat the oil. Add the red onion and garlic and cook for 3 to 4 minutes, stirring occasionally, until beginning to soften.

3. Add the sausage and cook for 2 to 3 minutes.

4. Add the wine, broth, tomato paste, and tomatoes and bring to a simmer. Cook, uncovered, for 10 minutes.

5. Add the basil and mussels to the pot, give everything a good toss, cover the pot, and cook for up to 10 minutes, until the mussels have steamed open. Discard any mussels that do not open.

6. Place the pasta in a large serving dish. Pour the sausage, mussels, and broth over the pasta. Give everything a good toss before serving.

PER SERVING Calories: 616; Total Carbohydrates: 68g; Sugar: 6g; Total Fat: 15g; Saturated Fat: 3g; Sodium: 909mg; Protein: 42g; Fiber: 13g

Poached Salmon with Dill Pickle Mayo

EGG-FREE GLUTEN-FREE

SERVES 4

PREP TIME:
10 minutes

COOK TIME:
10 minutes

INGREDIENT TIP: To make homemade egg-free mayonnaise, in a high-speed blender, combine 1 cup blanched almonds (soaked in water for 1 to 2 hours, rinsed, and drained), 1 cup neutral-flavored oil, 1 tablespoon distilled white vinegar, 2 teaspoons sugar, 2 teaspoons salt, and ¾ cup water. Blend until smooth.

The cooking method of poaching salmon in a foil pack creates less mess and doesn't make the whole house smell like fish. The dill pickle mayo complements the salmon perfectly. If you're lucky, you'll have some mayo left over to use as a condiment on a burger or sandwich.

4 (1-inch-thick) salmon fillets (about 1½ pounds)

Olive oil, for drizzling

Salt

Freshly ground black pepper

½ cup homemade egg-free mayonnaise (see tip) or store-bought egg-free mayonnaise

Grated zest of ½ lemon

Juice of ½ lemon

1 large dill pickle, finely chopped

1 teaspoon finely chopped scallion

1. Bring a large pot of water to a boil.

2. Cut four 10-by-18-inch sheets of heavy-duty aluminum foil. Place each salmon fillet on one sheet of foil and drizzle with oil. Season with salt and pepper. Fold the foil over the salmon to enclose it, pressing out any air. Fold the foil on the sides to seal the packets. Carefully drop the packets into the boiling water, cover the pot, and cook for about 10 minutes, just until firm to the touch.

3. In a small bowl, whisk the mayonnaise, lemon zest and juice, pickle, and scallion to combine. Season with salt and pepper.

4. Transfer each foil packet to a plate and carefully cut each open. Dollop the salmon with the dill pickle mayo.

PER SERVING Calories: 353; Total Carbohydrates: 2g; Sugar: 1g; Total Fat: 22g; Saturated Fat: 3g; Sodium: 471mg; Protein: 36g; Fiber: 1g

Seared Garlic Scallops and Linguine

EGG-FREE NUT-FREE

Fresh sea scallops cooked with garlic, parsley, and fresh lemon juice is a simple and delicious combination atop a bed of linguine. Use fresh pasta for an extra-special meal. Whether you use fresh or dried pasta, the starches from the pasta cooking liquid create a thick, creamy pan sauce without using a drop of cream.

SERVES 4

PREP TIME:
5 minutes

COOK TIME:
15 minutes

COOKING TIP:
To baste the scallops, tilt the pan slightly and use a spoon to scoop up the pan juices and drizzle them over the scallops.

Sea salt

12 ounces linguine

2 tablespoons canola oil

1 pound large sea scallops

Freshly ground black pepper

1 tablespoon minced garlic

¼ cup minced fresh parsley

2 tablespoons freshly squeezed lemon juice

1. Bring a large pot of salted water to a boil. Cook the pasta according to the package directions. Drain the pasta, reserving ⅓ cup of the cooking liquid.

2. Heat a large skillet over high heat until very hot. Add the oil and tilt the skillet to coat the bottom with the oil. Heat the oil for 30 seconds.

3. Pat the scallops dry with paper towels and season generously with salt and pepper. Sear the scallops for 2 minutes on one side, basting them with the pan juices (see tip). Flip the scallops and sear for 2 minutes on the other side.

4. During the last minute of cooking, add the garlic, parsley, and lemon juice to the skillet, continuing to baste the scallops with the pan juices.

5. Add the pasta to the skillet, along with the reserved cooking liquid. Give everything a good toss, season with salt and pepper, and divide among four serving plates.

PER SERVING Calories: 485; Total Carbohydrates: 68g; Sugar: 3g; Total Fat: 9g; Saturated Fat: 1g; Sodium: 250mg; Protein: 31g; Fiber: 3g

Crab Cakes with Lemon Aioli

MAKE GLUTEN-FREE NUT-FREE

SERVES 4

PREP TIME:
10 minutes

COOK TIME:
10 minutes

**SUBSTITUTION
TIP:** Use
gluten-free
bread crumbs
to make
this recipe
gluten-free.

Crab is a classic in these simple cakes, but pretty much any seafood can be used. As with the Fish Tacos with Cilantro-Lime Crema (page 96), the sauce really does make the dish here. Instead of using a dairy-free sour cream, however, this version is made with prepared mayonnaise spiked with fresh lemon juice. It is tangy and delicious.

2 scallions, white and green parts, trimmed and thinly sliced

2 garlic cloves, minced, plus 1 teaspoon minced garlic

1 pound lump crabmeat, picked over for shells

1 cup fresh bread crumbs

1 large egg white

¼ teaspoon Old Bay seasoning

¼ teaspoon sea salt

¼ teaspoon freshly ground black pepper

⅓ cup mayonnaise

2 tablespoons freshly squeezed lemon juice

2 tablespoons canola oil

1 mint sprig, leaves removed and roughly chopped

1. In a small bowl, stir together the scallions, 2 minced garlic cloves, crabmeat, bread crumbs, egg white, Old Bay seasoning, salt, and pepper. Form the mixture into 8 cakes. Set aside to firm up and allow the flavors to come together.

2. In a small bowl, whisk the mayonnaise, lemon juice, and remaining 1 teaspoon minced garlic to combine. Cover and refrigerate until ready to serve.

3. Heat a large skillet over medium-high heat. Pour in the oil and add the crab cakes. Fry the cakes for 4 to 5 minutes per side until a golden crust forms.

4. To serve, drizzle with the lemon aioli and garnish with mint.

PER SERVING Calories: 338; Total Carbohydrates: 27g; Sugar: 3g; Total Fat: 24g; Saturated Fat: 2g; Sodium: 1,105mg; Protein: 21g; Fiber: 2g

Fish Tacos with Cilantro-Lime Crema

GLUTEN-FREE **MAKE EGG-FREE** **MAKE NUT-FREE**

SERVES 4

PREP TIME:
10 minutes

COOK TIME:
5 minutes

COOKING
TIP: I use an
immersion
blender when
mixing smaller
amounts of
ingredients,
but a regular
countertop
blender will
also work here.

What makes these tacos shine is the tangy crema.

FOR THE FISH

2 tablespoons canola oil

1 teaspoon ground cumin

1 teaspoon smoked paprika

1 teaspoon dried oregano

½ teaspoon sea salt

½ teaspoon freshly
ground black pepper

1 pound mahi-mahi, swordfish,
or other firm white fish

FOR THE CILANTRO-LIME CREMA

½ cup store-bought egg-free
mayonnaise or homemade
egg-free mayonnaise (see
Ingredient Tip, page 93)

½ cup Dairy-Free Sour Cream
(page 173), or store-bought
dairy-free sour cream

Grated zest of 1 lime

Juice of 1 lime

½ cup roughly chopped
fresh cilantro

½ small jalapeño pepper,
seeded

FOR SERVING

8 (6-inch) corn tortillas

1 cup pico de gallo

1 cup shredded green cabbage

1. **To make the fish:** In a shallow dish, mix the oil, cumin, paprika, oregano, salt, and pepper. Add the mahi-mahi and gently toss to coat.

2. Preheat a grill pan over medium-high heat. Add the mahi-mahi and cook for 4 to 5 minutes, turning as needed, just until cooked through. Break the fish into bite-size pieces.

3. **To make the crema:** In a blender, combine the mayonnaise, sour cream, lime zest and juice, cilantro, and jalapeño. Puree until smooth.

4. **To serve:** Top each tortilla with a few pieces of mahi-mahi, a scoop of pico de gallo, a pinch of shredded cabbage, and a drizzle of crema.

PER SERVING Calories: 412; Total Carbohydrates: 31g; Sugar: 5g; Total Fat: 21g;
Saturated Fat: 10g; Sodium: 795mg; Protein: 27g; Fiber: 5g

Tuna Casserole

SERVES 4

PREP TIME:
15 minutes

COOK TIME:
30 minutes

INGREDIENT TIP: Choose solid albacore tuna, which has larger pieces and a mild flavor perfect for this recipe.

This comforting casserole is made with chicken broth, nut milk, and dairy-free butter. A splash of the noodles' cooking liquid thickens the sauce.

3 tablespoons dairy-free butter (such as Earth Balance Buttery Spread), divided

Sea salt

12 ounces egg noodles or gluten-free pasta

1 cup minced onion

¼ cup minced celery

2 tablespoons all-purpose flour or gluten-free flour blend

1 cup chicken broth

1 cup Plain Nut Milk (page 22), made with almonds or cashews

1 cup frozen peas, thawed

2 (5-ounce) cans tuna, drained

Freshly ground black pepper

1 cup wheat or gluten-free bread crumbs

1. Preheat the oven to 350°F. Coat the interior of a 2-quart casserole dish with 1 tablespoon of the butter.

2. Bring a large pot of salted water to a boil. Cook the egg noodles according to the package directions. Drain the noodles, reserving ½ cup of the cooking liquid.

3. While the pasta cooks, in another large pot over medium heat, melt the remaining 2 tablespoons butter. Add onion and celery and cook for 5 to 7 minutes, until soft. Stir in flour and cook for 1 minute.

4. Pour in the broth and nut milk and bring to a simmer. Cook for 2 to 3 minutes, stirring occasionally, until thick and bubbling. Stir in the reserved cooking liquid.

5. Fold in the peas, tuna, and cooked pasta. Season with salt and pepper. Spread the tuna and noodles into the prepared casserole dish. Top with the bread crumbs.

6. Bake for 15 to 17 minutes, until the top is golden brown.

PER SERVING Calories: 546; Total Carbohydrates: 74g; Sugar: 6g; Total Fat: 13g; Saturated Fat: 3g; Sodium: 535mg; Protein: 33g; Fiber: 6g

Pork and Beef

➤ MEATBALL WRAPS WITH TZATZIKI, PAGE 107

Pepperoni, Red Onion, and Cherry Tomato Pizza

MAKE ALLERGEN-FREE MAKE EGG-FREE MAKE GLUTEN-FREE NUT-FREE

SERVES 4

PREP TIME:
10 minutes

COOK TIME:
12 minutes

**SUBSTITUTION
TIP:** To make
this gluten- and
allergen-free,
use a
gluten-free
pizza crust
made with-
out eggs.

Combining Tofu Ricotta (page 29) with dairy-free mozzarella makes this pizza especially creamy and delicious. Pepperoni, onion, tomatoes, and fresh herbs are a simple but winning flavor combination. I like using a cast-iron skillet and fresh pizza dough for a deep-dish option—just remember to par-bake the crust for 10 minutes before proceeding with the recipe. Enjoy it with a nice bottle of red wine.

1 (12-inch) prepared pizza crust

1 cup Pomodoro Sauce (page 177) or store-bought marinara sauce

2 tablespoons minced fresh herbs (such as basil and oregano)

1 cup Tofu Ricotta (page 29)

1 cup shredded dairy-free mozzarella (such as Follow Your Heart)

16 slices good-quality pepperoni

1 small red onion, halved and thinly sliced

¼ cup pitted black olives (such as Kalamata)

½ cup halved cherry tomatoes

1. Preheat the oven to 400°F.

2. Place the pizza crust on a large pan and spread the sauce over the crust. Sprinkle with the fresh herbs.

3. Drop the tofu ricotta by the tablespoon over the entire pizza and top with the mozzarella.

4. Layer the pepperoni, red onion, olives, and cherry tomatoes on the pizza.

5. Bake for 10 to 12 minutes, until the sauce is hot and bubbling and the crust begins to brown.

PER SERVING Calories: 411; Total Carbohydrates: 30g; Sugar: 10g; Total Fat: 28g; Saturated Fat: 12g; Sodium: 1361mg; Protein: 12g; Fiber: 5g

Carnitas Tacos

ALLERGEN-FREE EGG-FREE GLUTEN-FREE NUT-FREE

SERVES 6

PREP TIME:
10 minutes

COOK TIME:
2 hours
15 minutes

COOKING TIP:
To make this in a slow cooker, sear the meat, then transfer it to a slow cooker along with the spices, onion, garlic, and broth. Cover and cook on low for 8 to 10 hours, or on high for 4 to 6 hours.

My kids' school is predominantly Hispanic, so when holidays roll around, many bake sale items are upstaged by the most amazing Mexican-inspired foods—carnitas, barbacoa, tamales—it's all so delicious! Carnitas tacos are one of my favorites. Although this recipe takes a long time to cook, only 15 minutes of it is active time.

1 (1½-pound) boneless pork shoulder, cut into 1-inch chunks

Sea salt

Freshly ground black pepper

2 tablespoons canola oil

1 tablespoon ground cumin

2 teaspoons dried oregano

1¼ teaspoons ground cinnamon

1 teaspoon ground coriander

⅛ teaspoon ground cloves

Grated zest and juice of 1 orange

1 red onion, halved and sliced

4 garlic cloves, roughly chopped

2 cups chicken broth

12 (6-inch) corn tortillas

1 bunch radishes, thinly sliced

2 cups shredded green cabbage

1 avocado, peeled, halved, pitted, and sliced

2 limes, cut into wedges

1. Preheat the oven to 325°F.

2. Season the pork on all sides with salt and pepper.

3. In a Dutch oven or large oven-safe skillet with a lid over medium-high heat, heat the oil. Add the pork and sear for 10 to 15 minutes on all sides until well browned.

4. Add the cumin, oregano, cinnamon, coriander, cloves, orange zest and juice, red onion, garlic, and broth. Bring to a simmer. Cover the Dutch oven and transfer it to the oven.

5. Roast for 2 hours until the pork is tender. Shred the meat with a fork and serve in the corn tortillas. Top with radish slices, cabbage, and avocado and serve with lime wedges for squeezing.

PER SERVING Calories: 543; Total Carbohydrates: 30g; Sugar: 3g; Total Fat: 36g; Saturated Fat: 10g; Sodium: 376mg; Protein: 25g; Fiber: 7g

Creamy Tomato and Sausage Penne

EGG-FREE GLUTEN-FREE MAKE NUT-FREE

SERVES 4

PREP TIME:
10 minutes

COOK TIME:
25 minutes

INGREDIENT TIP: Red lentil penne pasta is available at Trader Joe's, Whole Foods, and other grocery stores, as well as online.

The first time I used pasta made from red lentil flour, I was amazed at its ability to create a rich, creamy sauce that bound the entire dish together. It is gluten-free and packed with protein!

8 ounces spicy Italian sausage, casings removed

1 red onion, diced

4 garlic cloves, roughly chopped

1 (15-ounce) can plum tomatoes, hand crushed, with juice

4 cups chicken broth

12 ounces red lentil penne pasta

½ cup roughly chopped fresh basil

¼ cup Plant-Based Parmesan (page 27), for serving (optional)

1. Heat a large pot over medium-high heat. Add the sausage and cook for 2 to 3 minutes, until it renders some of its fat but is not yet cooked through.

2. Add the onion and garlic and sauté for 1 to 2 minutes.

3. Add the tomatoes, broth, and pasta and bring to a simmer. Cover the pot and cook for 20 minutes.

4. Stir in the basil. Let the dish rest for a few minutes to thicken before serving, sprinkled with the Parmesan (if using).

PER SERVING Calories: 488; Total Carbohydrates: 67g; Sugar: 8g; Total Fat: 10g; Saturated Fat: 2g; Sodium: 1,118mg; Protein: 32g; Fiber: 8g

Coconut-Ginger Pork Tenderloin Skewers

ALLERGEN-FREE **EGG-FREE** **GLUTEN-FREE** **NUT-FREE**

SERVES 4

PREP TIME:
5 minutes,
plus at least
15 minutes
to marinate

COOK TIME:
15 minutes

SERVING TIP:
These skewers
are delicious
over an herb
salad. Toss
together ½ cup
each of fresh
mint leaves,
chopped fresh
basil and cilan-
tro, and 4 cups
torn butter
lettuce. Make a
vinaigrette with
2 tablespoons
freshly
squeezed
lime juice,
2 tablespoons
canola oil, and
1 teaspoon
honey. Season
with salt and
pepper.

Creamy coconut milk, fragrant ginger, and pungent spices marry beautifully in this marinade for pork tenderloin. This dish can be prepared in the oven or outside over a grill, and makes excellent leftovers—so whip up a double batch!

½ cup coconut milk

2 tablespoons roughly chopped peeled fresh ginger

1 shallot, roughly chopped

1 tablespoon brown sugar

2 teaspoons ground coriander

1 teaspoon sea salt

½ teaspoon ground cumin

¼ teaspoon cayenne pepper

1 (1½-pound) pork tenderloin, cut into 2-inch pieces

1. Preheat the oven to 400°F. Line a sheet pan with parchment paper.

2. In a blender, combine the coconut milk, ginger, shallot, brown sugar, coriander, salt, cumin, and cayenne. Puree until smooth.

3. Place the pork in a large bowl, pour the marinade over, and let rest for at least 15 minutes, or cover and refrigerate for up to 8 hours.

4. Thread the pork onto skewers and transfer to the prepared sheet pan.

5. Bake for 15 minutes, or until cooked through but still tender.

PER SERVING Calories: 279; Total Carbohydrates: 5g; Sugar: 3g; Total Fat: 15g; Saturated Fat: 8g; Sodium: 594mg; Protein: 37g; Fiber: 1g

Pork Marsala

EGG-FREE   MAKE ALLERGEN-FREE   MAKE GLUTEN-FREE   NUT-FREE

SERVES 4

PREP TIME:
10 minutes

COOK TIME:
25 minutes

The creamy, comforting flavors of pork Marsala usually come from butter and flour. This version opts for neutral-flavored canola oil to brown the meat, and all-purpose or gluten-free flour can be used for thickening. Use a good-quality chicken broth or make your own from roasted chicken bones—its flavor really makes the sauce.

3 tablespoons canola oil, divided

4 boneless pork loin chops, pounded to about ½-inch thickness

Sea salt

Freshly ground black pepper

2 tablespoons all-purpose flour or gluten-free flour blend

2 cups sliced mushrooms

½ yellow onion, minced

1 garlic clove, minced

1 teaspoon minced fresh thyme leaves

½ cup Marsala wine

½ cup chicken broth

1. Heat a large skillet over medium-high heat until hot. Pour in 2 tablespoons of the oil and tilt the skillet to coat the bottom with oil.

2. Pat the pork dry with a paper towels and season the pork with salt and pepper. Sprinkle the chops lightly with the flour, shaking off any excess. Place the pork in the skillet and cook for 3 minutes per side. Remove the pork from the skillet.

3. Add the remaining 1 tablespoon oil to the skillet along with the mushrooms. Sauté for about 4 minutes, until the mushrooms are browned.

4. Add the onion, garlic, and thyme to the skillet and cook for 30 seconds. Deglaze the pan with the wine, scraping up the browned bits from the bottom with a wooden spoon. Add the broth and bring to a simmer.

5. Return the pork chops to the skillet, cover, and finish cooking for 10 minutes, until the liquid is reduced by half.

PER SERVING Calories: 339; Total Carbohydrates: 8g; Sugar: 2g; Total Fat: 22g; Saturated Fat: 5g; Sodium: 581mg; Protein: 23g; Fiber: 1g

Rustic Italian Meatballs

MAKE GLUTEN-FREE **MAKE NUT-FREE**

SERVES 4

PREP TIME:
10 minutes

COOK TIME:
30 minutes

Parmesan and milk are often used in commercially prepared meatballs you would order in a restaurant or snag from the freezer section of the grocery store. Fortunately, soy milk or another dairy-free milk stands in easily for dairy, and fresh herbs and spices bring plenty of flavor to these meatballs.

2 slices white or gluten-free bread, torn into pieces

½ cup unsweetened plain Soy Milk (page 24) or store-bought soy milk

1 small yellow onion, minced

4 garlic cloves, minced

1 large egg, whisked

2 tablespoons minced fresh parsley

1 teaspoon minced fresh thyme leaves

1 teaspoon minced fresh oregano leaves

1 teaspoon ground fennel seed

1 teaspoon sea salt

½ teaspoon freshly ground black pepper

⅛ teaspoon red pepper flakes

12 ounces ground beef

12 ounces ground pork

2 tablespoons extra-virgin olive oil

3 cups Pomodoro Sauce (page 177) or good-quality store-bought marinara sauce

¼ cup finely sliced fresh basil

½ cup Plant-Based Parmesan (page 27; optional)

1. Preheat the oven to 425°F.

2. In a small bowl, soak the bread in the soy milk for 1 minute. Remove the bread and squeeze out most of the excess moisture.

3. In a large bowl, mix together the soaked bread, onion, garlic, egg, parsley, thyme, oregano, fennel seed, salt, black pepper, and red pepper flakes.

4. Add the ground beef and ground pork to the bowl and use your hands to thoroughly mix the ingredients. Shape the mixture into 8 to 12 large balls.

CONTINUED ➤

5. Heat a large oven-safe skillet over medium-high heat. Pour the oil into the skillet and tilt the skillet to coat the bottom in oil.

6. Place the meatballs in the skillet and fry for about 10 minutes, gently browning on all sides. Pour in the sauce and transfer the skillet to the oven.

7. Bake for 15 to 18 minutes, until the sauce is bubbling and the meatballs are cooked to an internal temperature of 160°F and tender.

8. Top with the basil and Parmesan (if using) to serve.

PER SERVING Calories: 528; Total Carbohydrates: 12g; Sugar: 5g; Total Fat: 42g; Saturated Fat: 14g; Sodium: 893mg; Protein: 26g; Fiber: 2g

Meatball Wraps with Tzatziki

MAKE GLUTEN-FREE NUT-FREE

SERVES 4

PREP TIME:
10 minutes

COOK TIME:
20 minutes

**VARIATION
TIP:** Use butter
lettuce leaves
instead of torti-
llas for
a low-carb,
gluten-free
option.

Tzatziki, with its cooling mint and cucumber flavors, provides the perfect complement to the full flavor of these lamb meatballs wrapped in soft flour tortillas. If you cannot find ground lamb, ground beef is a reasonable substitute.

1 plum tomato, finely diced

½ cup minced red onion

1 tablespoon minced garlic

1 large egg, whisked

2 tablespoons minced
   fresh parsley

1 tablespoon minced
   fresh oregano leaves

1 teaspoon sea salt

½ teaspoon freshly
   ground black pepper

1½ pounds ground lamb

4 (10-inch) flour tortillas

½ red onion, thinly sliced

½ cucumber, thinly sliced

1 cup arugula

¼ cup fresh mint leaves

1 cup Tzatziki (page 178)

1. Preheat the oven to 400°F.

2. In a large bowl, stir together the tomato, minced red onion, garlic, egg, parsley, oregano, salt, and pepper.

3. Add the ground lamb and use your hands to thoroughly mix the ingredients. Shape the mixture into 8 meatballs. Place the meatballs on a sheet pan.

4. Bake for 20 minutes, or until lightly browned and cooked to an internal temperature of 160°F.

5. To serve, place 2 meatballs on each tortilla. Top with sliced red onion, cucumber, arugula, mint, and a generous spoonful of tzatziki.

PER SERVING Calories: 603; Total Carbohydrates: 19g; Sugar: 5g; Total Fat: 47g; Saturated Fat: 18g; Sodium: 959mg; Protein: 29g; Fiber: 2g

Beefy Baked Nachos

EGG-FREE GLUTEN-FREE MAKE VEGAN

SERVES 4

PREP TIME:
10 minutes

COOK TIME:
15 minutes

VARIATION TIP:
If you aren't
into ground
beef, swap
it for ground
or shredded
chicken or even
mushrooms
for a vegan
variation.

Making nachos is one of the fastest ways to bring delicious comfort food to the table for your sweatpants-bedecked enjoyment. You can make a nacho plate into a personalized meal for yourself and others by preparing a handful of optional toppings.

8 ounces ground beef

1 tablespoon chili powder or dairy-free taco seasoning

Nonstick cooking spray

½ (18-ounce) bag corn tortilla chips

1 cup dairy-free Cheddar shreds

1 cup canned vegetarian refried beans (optional)

1 cup Nacho Cheese (page 181)

TOPPINGS (OPTIONAL)

Diced tomato

Guacamole

Sliced jalapeño pepper

Salsa

Dairy-Free Sour Cream (page 173) or store-bought dairy-free sour cream

1. Place a large skillet over medium-high heat, add the ground beef and chili powder, and sauté for about 8 minutes, until cooked through and no longer pink. Set aside.

2. Preheat the oven to 350°F.

3. Lightly spray a baking sheet with cooking spray and arrange a layer of tortilla chips on it, overlapping a little. Top the chips with half the cheese, the ground beef, refried beans (if using), and remaining cheese shreds.

4. Bake for 15 minutes, until the cheese is melted and the nachos are heated through.

5. Transfer the nachos to a serving plate and drizzle with the nacho cheese.

6. Serve with toppings, as desired.

PER SERVING Calories: 616; Total Carbohydrates: 69g; Sugar: 2g; Total Fat: 27g; Saturated Fat: 7g; Sodium: 839mg; Protein: 25g; Fiber: 6g

Shepherd's Pie

EGG-FREE   GLUTEN-FREE   MAKE ALLERGEN-FREE   MAKE NUT-FREE

SERVES 4

PREP TIME:
10 minutes

COOK TIME:
40 minutes

SUBSTITUTION TIP: To make the recipe nut-free and allergen-free, use an unsweetened plain rice milk to make the potatoes and ensure that the dairy-free butter does not contain soy.

My favorite dinners are the ones I can prepare ahead, leave in the refrigerator, then simply pop into the oven at the end of a long day. This comforting shepherd's pie contains all the classic ingredients of the original, with a few minor tweaks to make it dairy-free.

2 tablespoons canola oil

1 yellow onion, diced

2 carrots, diced

1 cup finely chopped mushrooms

1 celery stalk, minced

2 garlic cloves, minced

1½ pounds ground beef or lamb

1 teaspoon minced fresh thyme leaves

1 teaspoon minced fresh rosemary leaves

1 cup frozen peas, thawed

1 tablespoon tomato paste

½ teaspoon sea salt, plus more for seasoning

Freshly ground black pepper

2 cups water

4 tablespoons (½ stick) dairy-free butter (such as Earth Balance Buttery Spread), divided

2 cups instant mashed potato flakes

1 cup Plain Nut Milk (page 22), or store-bought dairy-free milk

1. Preheat the oven to 425°F.

2. In a large oven-safe skillet over medium heat, heat the oil. Add the onion, carrots, mushrooms, celery, and garlic. Cook for 10 minutes, until soft and fragrant.

3. Push the vegetables to the side of the skillet and add the ground beef, thyme, and rosemary. Cook for about 10 minutes, until the beef is just cooked through. Stir in the peas and tomato paste and season generously with salt and pepper.

4. While the beef cooks, in a medium pot over medium-high heat, combine the water, salt, and 3 tablespoons of the butter. Bring to a simmer. Stir in the potato flakes and nut milk just until combined.

5. Spread the mashed potatoes over the beef mixture. Melt remaining 1 tablespoon butter and brush the potatoes with it. Transfer the skillet to oven.

6. Bake for 15 minutes, or until the potatoes are lightly browned.

PER SERVING Calories: 563; Total Carbohydrates: 34g; Sugar: 6g; Total Fat: 31g; Saturated Fat: 8g; Sodium: 601mg; Protein: 39g; Fiber: 6g

Meatloaf

MAKE GLUTEN-FREE   NUT-FREE

SERVES 8

PREP TIME:
10 minutes

COOK TIME:
1 hour, plus
10 minutes
to rest

**INGREDIENT
TIP:** Onion,
carrot, and
celery are often
used together
in traditional
French cooking
and are referred
to as mirepoix
(meer-pwah).

Some meatloaf recipes use milk-soaked bread crumbs or add Parmesan cheese. This version is just as delicious, but it uses diced tomatoes to keep the meatloaf moist. I recommend baking the meatloaf directly on a sheet pan instead of in a loaf pan, which helps it brown nicely all around.

1 tablespoon extra-virgin olive oil

1 yellow onion, minced

1 carrot, minced

1 celery stalk, minced

4 garlic cloves, minced

1 teaspoon minced fresh rosemary leaves

1 teaspoon minced fresh thyme leaves

Pinch red pepper flakes

½ cup toasted bread crumbs or gluten-free bread crumbs

1 large egg

1 teaspoon sea salt

½ teaspoon freshly ground black pepper

2 plum tomatoes, finely diced (about ½ cup)

2 pounds ground beef

½ cup ketchup, plus more for serving

1. Preheat the oven to 400°F. Line a sheet pan with parchment paper.

2. In a large skillet over medium heat, heat the oil. Add the onion, carrot, celery, garlic, rosemary, thyme, and red pepper flakes. Cook for about 10 minutes, until soft. Let cool briefly.

3. In a large bowl, whisk the bread crumbs, egg, salt, and pepper to combine. Add the tomatoes and cooked vegetables and stir until thoroughly mixed.

4. Add the ground beef and use your hands to mix the ingredients just until combined. Spread the mixture into a 9-inch loaf pan to form, then invert it onto the prepared sheet pan. Drizzle with the ketchup.

5. Bake, uncovered, for 45 to 50 minutes or until the meatloaf is cooked to an internal temperature of 160°F.

6. Let the meatloaf rest for 10 minutes, then slice into slightly larger than 1-inch-thick slices. Serve with additional ketchup.

PER SERVING Calories: 310; Total Carbohydrates: 13g; Sugar: 6g; Total Fat: 20g; Saturated Fat: 7g; Sodium: 524mg; Protein: 22g; Fiber: 1g

Steak au Poivre

EGG-FREE GLUTEN-FREE MAKE ALLERGEN-FREE NUT-FREE

SERVES 4

PREP TIME:
5 minutes

COOK TIME:
10 minutes

VARIATION TIP:
For a lighter pan sauce that also tastes amazing with peppercorn-crusted steak, skip the brandy, dairy-free butter, and coconut cream. Add 1 cup dry red wine and 2 thyme sprigs to the skillet after cooking the steak and cook for about 10 minutes, until reduced to about ⅓ cup.

Coating steak in freshly ground peppercorns, then pan searing is my favorite preparation method for steak because the pepper forms a nice crust on the browned meat. The traditional French recipe for peppercorn-crusted steak is called *steak au poivre*, or pepper steak, and is often served with a pan sauce made of heavy cream. This version creates a luxurious sauce with cognac, dairy-free butter, and coconut cream.

4 (4- to 6-ounce) filet mignon steaks

¼ cup peppercorns, coarsely ground

½ teaspoon sea salt

1 tablespoon canola oil

¼ cup cognac or another brandy

2 tablespoons dairy-free butter (such as Earth Balance Buttery Spread)

¼ cup canned coconut cream

1. Heat a large skillet over medium-high heat until very hot.

2. While the skillet heats, pat the steaks dry with paper towels and season them with the pepper and salt.

3. Pour the oil into the hot skillet and tilt the skillet to coat the bottom with oil. Add the steaks to the skillet and sear for 3 minutes per side for medium-rare. Transfer the steaks to a cutting board to rest.

4. Carefully pour the cognac into the pan and return it to the heat. Simmer for 2 minutes, until reduced to about 2 tablespoons. Whisk in the butter and cook for 1 minute. Stir in the coconut cream and simmer just until heated through and thick.

5. To serve, place the steaks on individual plates and drizzle with the peppercorn pan sauce.

PER SERVING Calories: 483; Total Carbohydrates: 2g; Sugar: 1g; Total Fat: 29g; Saturated Fat: 11g; Sodium: 400mg; Protein: 49g; Fiber: 1g

Beef Stroganoff

MAKE EGG-FREE MAKE GLUTEN-FREE NUT-FREE

SERVES 5

PREP TIME:
10 minutes

COOK TIME:
30 minutes

Don't skip the "secret" ingredient: demi-glace. You can purchase it online or in well-stocked grocery stores, or make your own. For an egg- and gluten-free meal, skip the egg noodles and serve with my Mashed Potatoes (page 80) instead.

Sea salt

12 ounces egg noodles or gluten-free noodles

1 tablespoon canola oil

1 pound boneless rib-eye steak, thinly sliced on a bias

Freshly ground black pepper

1 yellow onion, halved and thinly sliced

1 tablespoon dairy-free butter (such as Earth Balance Buttery Spread)

2 cups sliced cremini mushrooms

¼ cup brandy

1 cup beef broth

3 tablespoons demi-glace

1 bay leaf

1 teaspoon whole-grain mustard

½ cup Dairy-Free Sour Cream (page 173) or store-bought dairy-free sour cream

2 tablespoons roughly chopped fresh parsley

1. Bring a large pot of salted water to a boil. Cook the noodles according to the package directions. Drain and set aside.

2. While the noodles cook, heat a large skillet over medium-high heat. Pour in the oil and tilt the skillet to coat the bottom with oil.

3. Pat the rib-eye dry with paper towels, thoroughly season with salt and pepper, and hot place in the hot skillet. Quickly sauté for 3 to 5 minutes total just until cooked through. Transfer the steak to a dish.

4. Return the skillet to the heat and add the onion. Cook for about 5 minutes, until the onion begins to soften. Push the onion to the side of the skillet and add the butter to melt.

5. Add the mushrooms and let sear for about 10 minutes, until well browned.

6. Carefully pour in the brandy and deglaze the pan, scraping up the browned bits from the bottom with a wooden spoon.

7. Return the steak and any accumulated juices to the skillet. Stir in the broth, demi-glace, bay leaf, and mustard and simmer for 5 minutes.

8. Remove the skillet from the heat, remove and discard the bay leaf, and stir in the sour cream until integrated into the sauce. Stir in the cooked egg noodles.

9. Garnish with parsley to serve.

PER SERVING Calories: 643; Total Carbohydrates: 54g; Sugar: 5g; Total Fat: 30g; Saturated Fat: 12g; Sodium: 358mg; Protein: 37g; Fiber: 3g

Poultry

Chicken in White Wine

SERVES 4

PREP TIME:
5 minutes

COOK TIME:
30 minutes

COOKING TIP:
Some recipes for coq au vin call for using skin-on chicken pieces, but I found that, even after a perfect sear, the skin becomes slimy after being cooked in wine. Not too appetizing!

This classic French recipe for coq au vin can be made with red or white wine, but I prefer the subtlety of white wine. Plus, white wine doesn't stain the chicken purple. The sauce is typically finished with butter, but in this version, I reduce it further on the stovetop and whisk in a dairy-free butter to yield a rich, velvety sauce.

1 tablespoon canola oil

1 pound boneless, skinless chicken thighs

Sea salt

Freshly ground black pepper

1 cup minced yellow onion

2 garlic cloves, smashed

1 thyme sprig

1½ cups dry white wine

1 cup low-sodium chicken broth

2 tablespoons dairy-free butter (such as Earth Balance Buttery Spread)

1. Heat a large pot over medium-high heat, then pour in the oil.

2. Pat the chicken thighs dry with paper towels and generously season with salt and pepper. Add the chicken to the hot oil and sear for about 2 minutes per side just until browned but not cooked through. Transfer to a dish.

3. Add the onion and garlic to the pot and cook for 3 minutes just until beginning to soften. Add the thyme.

4. Return the chicken and any accumulated juices to the pot. Add the wine and broth. Bring to a gentle simmer and cook for 15 minutes, or until the chicken is cooked through and no longer pink. Transfer the chicken to a serving platter.

5. Simmer the remaining pot liquid for about 8 minutes, until it has reduced to about 1 cup. Remove and discard the thyme. Whisk in the butter. Pour the sauce over the chicken to serve.

PER SERVING Calories: 302; Total Carbohydrates: 6g; Sugar: 2g; Total Fat: 14g; Saturated Fat: 3g; Sodium: 237mg; Protein: 23g; Fiber: 1g

Barbecue Chicken Ranch Pizza

EGG-FREE **MAKE GLUTEN-FREE** **NUT-FREE**

SERVES 2

PREP TIME:
10 minutes

COOK TIME:
12 minutes

INGREDIENT TIP: When I'm not making it from scratch, my favorite brand of barbecue sauce is Stubb's. It is naturally gluten-free and has only 2 to 4 grams of sugar per serving depending on which variety you choose, which is a fraction of the sugar found in other brands.

This recipe title sounds like junk food heaven, but this pizza is actually pretty healthy. Grilled chicken, a low-sugar barbecue sauce, and dairy-free ranch dressing atop a whole-grain crust make for a surprisingly sensible but yummy dinner. I suggest adding some thinly sliced spinach and scallions for color and texture, if you're so inclined.

1 (12-inch) prepared whole-grain or gluten-free pizza crust

1 cup low-sugar barbecue sauce (such as Stubb's; see Ingredient Tip)

8 ounces grilled chicken, sliced

½ red onion, thinly sliced

½ cup Ranch Dressing (page 170)

½ cup thinly sliced fresh spinach (optional)

1 scallion, white and green parts, trimmed and thinly sliced on a bias (optional)

1. Preheat the oven to 400°F.

2. Place the pizza crust on a large sheet pan and spread the barbecue sauce over the top. Layer the chicken and red onion over the sauce.

3. Bake for 10 to 12 minutes, until the sauce is hot and bubbling and the crust begins to brown. Remove the pizza from the oven.

4. Drizzle the pizza with the ranch dressing and sprinkle with the spinach (if using) and scallions (if using) before serving.

PER SERVING Calories: 443; Total Carbohydrates: 44g; Sugar: 21g; Total Fat: 4g; Saturated Fat: 1g; Sodium: 1,670mg; Protein: 58g; Fiber: 2g

Green Chile Chicken Enchiladas

ALLERGEN-FREE · EGG-FREE · GLUTEN-FREE · NUT-FREE

SERVES 4

PREP TIME:
10 minutes

COOK TIME:
35 minutes,
plus
5 minutes
to rest

COOKING TIP:
Prepare this
dish ahead and
refrigerate until
ready to bake.
Add 10 minutes
to the cook-
ing time.

In this timeless Mexican dish, tangy green sauce envelops enchiladas stuffed with chicken, peppers, onion, garlic, and dairy-free cream cheese.

1 tablespoon canola oil, plus more for coating the casserole

1 pound boneless, skinless chicken thighs, diced

Sea salt

Freshly ground black pepper

1 green bell pepper, thinly sliced

1 small yellow onion, halved and thinly sliced

1 tablespoon minced garlic

1 (8-ounce) container dairy-free cream cheese

12 (6-inch) corn tortillas

1 (15-ounce) can green chile enchilada sauce

1. Preheat the oven to 375°F. Lightly coat a 2-quart casserole dish with oil.

2. In a large skillet over medium-high heat, heat the oil. Season the chicken with salt and pepper and add it to the skillet. Cook for 2 minutes, stirring occasionally.

3. Add the bell pepper and onion to the skillet. Cook for 7 to 8 minutes, stirring occasionally, until the vegetables are soft and the chicken is cooked through and no longer pink. Add the garlic and cook for 30 seconds until fragrant.

4. Stir in the cream cheese, giving everything a good toss to mix.

5. Heat the corn tortillas individually in the microwave for about 10 seconds each, or until they're pliable. Scoop a heaping ¼ cup of warm filling into a tortilla and roll into a cylinder. Place it in the casserole dish, seam-side down. Repeat with the remaining filling and tortillas. Pour the green chile sauce over the enchiladas.

6. Bake for 20 minutes, until the sauce is bubbling. Let rest for 5 minutes before serving.

PER SERVING Calories: 423; Total Carbohydrates: 20g; Sugar: 6g; Total Fat: 31g; Saturated Fat: 10g; Sodium: 1,304mg; Protein: 19g; Fiber: 1g

Pan-Seared Chicken with Mushrooms and Cream

ALLERGEN-FREE   EGG-FREE   GLUTEN-FREE   NUT-FREE

SERVES 4

PREP TIME:
5 minutes

COOK TIME:
15 minutes

COOKING TIP: Want even more mushroom-y goodness? Soak 1 ounce dried wild mushrooms in 1 cup boiling water for 10 minutes. Strain the mushrooms, reserving the broth for another use. Roughly chop the mushrooms and add them during the last minute of the fresh mushroom cooking time in step 3.

Decadent, creamy, and filled with umami flavors, this chicken dish is far greater than the sum of its parts. The recipe, inspired by the classic French recipe for mushrooms in port and cream, takes a fraction of the time the original does, and swaps butter and cream for canola oil and coconut cream for a comparable dairy-free option. Serve with the Vegetable Bake with Cayenne (page 77), or with a side of roasted potatoes.

2 tablespoons canola oil, divided

4 (4-ounce) boneless, skinless chicken thighs

Sea salt

Freshly ground black pepper

2 cups thinly sliced cremini mushrooms

1 small shallot, minced

¼ cup port

¼ cup canned coconut cream

1. Heat a large skillet over medium-high heat. Pour in 1 tablespoon of the oil and tilt the skillet to coat the bottom with oil.

2. Season the chicken on all sides with salt and pepper and add it to the hot skillet. Sear the chicken for 2 minutes per side until browned but not cooked through. Transfer to a dish.

3. Add the remaining 1 tablespoon oil to the skillet, along with the mushrooms and shallot. Cook for 5 minutes, until the mushrooms are deeply browned.

4. Carefully add the port to the skillet and cook for 1 minute to burn off some of the alcohol. Add the coconut cream and bring to a simmer.

5. Return the chicken and any accumulated juices to the skillet. Cook for about 2 minutes, until the chicken is cooked through and no longer pink and the sauce is thick.

PER SERVING Calories: 321; Total Carbohydrates: 5g; Sugar: 1g; Total Fat: 22g; Saturated Fat: 10g; Sodium: 161mg; Protein: 24g; Fiber: 0g

Creamy Coconut-Lime Chicken

ALLERGEN-FREE EGG-FREE GLUTEN-FREE NUT-FREE

SERVES 4

PREP TIME:
10 minutes

COOK TIME:
20 minutes

INGREDIENT TIP: For the best texture, purchase young, thin green beans, such as haricots verts, for this recipe.

This one-pan supper hits all the right notes. It's tangy, spicy, and creamy, with just a hint of sweetness. The flavor of the coconut milk is a welcome addition, so I don't recommend swapping it for another nondairy milk.

1 tablespoon canola oil

4 (6-ounce) boneless, skinless chicken breasts

Sea salt

Freshly ground black pepper

½ red onion, halved and thinly sliced

2 garlic cloves, smashed

1 teaspoon minced peeled fresh ginger

Pinch red pepper flakes

1 cup coconut milk

½ cup chicken broth

12 ounces green beans, trimmed

Grated zest of 1 lime

Juice of 1 lime

¼ cup roughly chopped fresh cilantro

1. In a large skillet over medium-high heat, heat the oil.

2. Pat the chicken dry with paper towels and season with salt and pepper. Add the chicken to the skillet and sear for 4 to 5 minutes on one side until well browned. Flip the chicken.

3. Add the red onion, garlic, ginger, and red pepper flakes to the skillet. Cook for 2 minutes until fragrant.

4. Add the coconut milk, broth, green beans, and lime zest. Simmer for 10 minutes, until the chicken is cooked through and no longer pink and the green beans are tender.

5. Stir in the lime juice and cilantro, and serve.

PER SERVING Calories: 390; Total Carbohydrates: 12g; Sugar: 4g; Total Fat: 20g; Saturated Fat: 13g; Sodium: 282mg; Protein: 43g; Fiber: 5g

Green Goddess Chicken

EGG-FREE   GLUTEN-FREE

SERVES 4

PREP TIME:
5 minutes

COOK TIME:
10 minutes

COOKING TIP:
Delicate fresh
herbs, such as
tarragon, lose
their flavor
when cooked
for prolonged
periods. Adding
the sauce at the
end of cooking
warms it gently
while preserv-
ing the flavor.

Originating in San Francisco in the 1920s, Green Goddess dressing was created by chef Philip Roemer of the Palace Hotel as a tribute to a play by the same name. The sauce is remarkably similar to the French *sauce au vert*, which also contains tarragon, lemon juice, and parsley. Whatever its origins, the bright springtime flavors in this dish are perfectly balanced by the creaminess of the cashew cream. You can also use another unsweetened dairy-free creamer instead of the cashew cream.

1 tablespoon canola oil

4 (6-ounce) boneless,
skinless chicken breasts

Sea salt

Freshly ground black pepper

1 small shallot, minced

¼ cup fresh parsley leaves
and tender stems

2 tablespoons minced
fresh chives

2 tablespoons minced
fresh tarragon

1 teaspoon freshly
squeezed lemon juice

¼ cup Cashew Cream (page 23)

¼ cup chicken broth

1. Heat a large skillet over medium-high heat. Pour in the oil and tilt the skillet to coat the bottom with oil.

2. Season the chicken on all sides with salt and pepper and place it in the skillet. Sear the chicken for 5 minutes on one side until well browned.

3. While the chicken cooks, in a blender, combine the shallot, parsley, chives, tarragon, lemon juice, cashew cream, and broth. Puree until smooth.

4. Flip the chicken and sear for 5 minutes on the other side until cooked through and no longer pink.

5. Add the herb dressing to the pan and cook just until warmed.

PER SERVING Calories: 253; Total Carbohydrates: 2g; Sugar: 1g; Total Fat: 10g; Saturated Fat: 4g; Sodium: 222mg; Protein: 40g; Fiber: 1g

Green Curry with Chicken and Eggplant

EGG-FREE GLUTEN-FREE NUT-FREE

SERVES 4

PREP TIME:
10 minutes

COOK TIME:
30 minutes

VARIATION TIP:
This recipe
uses chicken
and eggplant,
but feel free
to substi-
tute another
nonstarchy
vegetable you
may have on
hand, such
as asparagus,
broccoli,
cauliflower, or
green beans.

Curries are a quick and easy way to use extra produce or protein at the end of the week and pack a big flavor punch. Turmeric can be bitter to some, so use less if you are not accustomed to its unique flavor. Serve this curry over rice.

¼ cup coconut oil

1 pound boneless, skinless chicken thighs, cut into 1-inch pieces

½ onion, chopped

2 cups cubed eggplant

4 garlic cloves, minced

2 teaspoons green curry paste

1 teaspoon ground turmeric

1 teaspoon salt

½ to 1 teaspoon red pepper flakes (optional)

2 (13.5-ounce) cans full-fat coconut milk

1 to 2 teaspoons monk fruit extract (optional)

Grated zest of 1 lime (slice the lime and reserve for serving)

¼ cup thinly sliced fresh basil, mint, or cilantro

1. In a large stockpot or skillet over medium-high heat, heat the coconut oil. Add the chicken, onion, and eggplant and sauté for 5 to 6 minutes, or until the chicken is browned and the vegetables are just tender.

2. Stir in the garlic, curry paste, turmeric, salt, and red pepper flakes (if using). Sauté for 2 minutes, until very fragrant.

3. Add the coconut milk, monk fruit extract (if using), and lime zest and bring to a boil. Reduce the heat to low, cover the pot, and simmer for 15 to 20 minutes. Serve warm, garnished with lime slices and basil.

PER SERVING Calories: 658; Total Carbohydrates: 11g; Sugar: 2g; Total Fat: 59g; Saturated Fat: 49g; Sodium: 717mg; Protein: 27g; Fiber: 2g

Chicken Fettucine with Sundried Tomato Cream Sauce

ALLERGEN-FREE EGG-FREE MAKE GLUTEN-FREE NUT-FREE

SERVES 4

PREP TIME:
10 minutes

COOK TIME:
20 minutes

SUBSTITUTION TIP: To reduce the fat in this dish, use dry-packed sundried tomatoes.

Sundried tomatoes enliven this creamy chicken dish made with sautéed red onion, garlic, and fresh oregano. The creamy texture of the coconut cream works nicely in this dish, but its tropical undertones are completely upstaged by the pungent flavors of garlic and herbs. This dish is especially awesome served over the bed of fresh pasta.

Sea salt

12 ounces fettucine noodles or gluten-free pasta

1 tablespoon canola oil

1 pound boneless, skinless chicken pieces

Freshly ground black pepper

½ red onion, thinly sliced

2 garlic cloves, smashed

½ cup thinly sliced oil-packed sundried tomatoes, drained

2 teaspoons minced fresh oregano

1 cup chicken broth

¼ cup canned coconut cream

1 cup thinly sliced fresh spinach

¼ cup roughly chopped fresh basil

1. Bring a large pot of salted water to a boil. Cook the pasta according to the package instructions. Drain and set aside.

2. While the pasta cooks, heat a large skillet over medium-high heat. Pour in the oil and tilt the skillet to coat the bottom with oil.

3. Season the chicken on all sides with salt and pepper and add it to the skillet. Sear the chicken for 2 minutes per side.

4. Flip the chicken pieces and add the red onion, garlic, sundried tomatoes, oregano, and broth. Bring to a simmer and cook for 10 minutes, until the chicken is cooked through and no longer pink.

5. Stir in the coconut cream, and cook for another minute.

6. Just before serving, stir in the spinach and basil. Place the pasta in a serving dish and pour the chicken and sauce over the top.

PER SERVING Calories: 563; Total Carbohydrates: 71g; Sugar: 4g; Total Fat: 14g; Saturated Fat: 4g; Sodium: 358mg; Protein: 38g; Fiber: 5g

Cashew, Chicken, and Mango Stir-Fry

EGG-FREE GLUTEN-FREE

SERVES 4

PREP TIME:
5 minutes

COOK TIME:
15 minutes

COOKING TIP:
It's best to
have all of the
ingredients
measured
before you
start cooking,
because this
dish comes
together really
quickly!

I have been making some rendition of this dish for years. There's something about the spicy red pepper flakes, sweet mango, salty fish sauce, and crunchy snap peas that just works for me. It's naturally low in carbs, but you can serve it with steamed rice for a complete meal.

1 tablespoon canola oil

1 pound boneless, skinless
  chicken thighs, diced

2 tablespoons fish sauce

2 tablespoons freshly
  squeezed lime juice

1 tablespoon brown sugar

1 pound sugar snap peas,
  stringed and halved

2 garlic cloves, minced

⅛ teaspoon red pepper flakes

½ cup toasted cashews

1 mango, diced

1. Heat a large skillet over medium-high heat. Pour in the oil and tilt the skillet to coat the bottom with oil. Add the chicken thighs and cook for 6 to 8 minutes, stirring occasionally, just until cooked through. Transfer to a dish.

2. While the chicken cooks, in a small bowl, whisk the fish sauce, lime juice, and brown sugar. Set aside.

3. Add the snap peas to the skillet and cook for 2 to 3 minutes, until bright green.

4. Add the garlic and red pepper flakes and cook for about 30 seconds until fragrant.

5. Pour the fish sauce mixture into the skillet and return the chicken and any accumulated juices to the skillet as well. Cook for 30 seconds, then remove from the heat.

6. Carefully fold in the cashews and mango. Serve immediately.

PER SERVING Calories: 484; Total Carbohydrates: 31g; Sugar: 20g; Total Fat: 29g; Saturated Fat: 7g; Sodium: 789mg; Protein: 27g; Fiber: 5g

Chicken Tikka Masala

ALLERGEN-FREE   EGG-FREE   GLUTEN-FREE   NUT-FREE

SERVES 4

PREP TIME:
10 minutes

COOK TIME:
20 minutes

COOKING TIP:
This recipe
also works in
a slow cooker.
Combine all
the ingredients
except the
coconut cream
and cilantro,
cover, and cook
on low heat for
6 to 8 hours.
Stir in the coco-
nut cream and
cilantro just
before serving.

When I lived in England, tikka masala was my favorite thing to eat when we went out to the pub. I could find it right alongside bangers and mash and fish and chips, but it was far more flavorful and healthier, too. Not the history you envisioned from the name, right? Its origin is debated, but it remains a British favorite. Traditionally, the dish is thickened with yogurt and heavy cream, but this version uses coconut cream, which pairs well with the fragrant Indian spices.

1 tablespoon canola oil

1 yellow onion, diced

2 garlic cloves, minced

1 teaspoon minced
  peeled fresh ginger

1 teaspoon ground coriander

1 teaspoon ground cumin

1 teaspoon smoked paprika

⅛ teaspoon red pepper flakes

1 pound boneless, skinless
  chicken thighs

1 (15-ounce) can diced plum
  tomatoes, with juices

1 cup low-sodium chicken broth

Sea salt

Freshly ground black pepper

¼ cup canned coconut cream

¼ cup minced fresh cilantro

1 lime, cut into wedges

1. In a large skillet over medium heat, heat the oil. Add the onion, garlic, and ginger and cook for 5 minutes, until the onion has softened somewhat.

2. Add the coriander, cumin, paprika, and red pepper flakes to the skillet. Cook for 1 minute until fragrant.

3. Add the chicken to the skillet, along with the tomatoes and broth. Generously season with salt and pepper. Simmer for about 10 minutes, until the chicken is cooked through and no longer pink.

4. Remove the skillet from the heat and stir in the coconut cream. Garnish with the cilantro and serve with lime wedges for squeezing.

PER SERVING Calories: 347; Total Carbohydrates: 9g; Sugar: 5g; Total Fat: 25g; Saturated Fat: 9g; Sodium: 171mg; Protein: 22g; Fiber: 3g

Southwestern Chicken Casserole

ALLERGEN-FREE EGG-FREE GLUTEN-FREE NUT-FREE

SERVES 4

PREP TIME:
5 minutes

COOK TIME:
35 minutes

INGREDIENT TIP: I like to purchase a whole rotisserie chicken to use in this recipe. I have plenty left over for other meals and can use the bones to make stock.

This easy one-dish main dish is inspired by a stuffed chicken breast I enjoyed at a modern Mexican restaurant in Arizona. Stuffing individual chicken breasts can be time-consuming to make and a little fussy for my taste. Plus, the chicken easily dries out before the filling has a chance to cook. So, instead, I turned the idea into this creamy casserole. Serve with blue corn tortilla chips.

1 teaspoon canola oil

2 cups shredded cooked chicken breast

2 cups cooked white or brown rice

1 cup fresh corn kernels

¼ cup diced green chiles

¼ cup minced sundried tomatoes

1 cup Dairy-Free Sour Cream (page 173) or store-bought dairy-free sour cream

¼ cup minced fresh cilantro

Sea salt

Freshly ground black pepper

1. Preheat the oven to 400°F. Coat the interior of a 2-quart casserole dish with oil.

2. Add the chicken, rice, corn, chiles, tomatoes, and sour cream to the prepared dish and gently toss to mix. Flatten with the back of a spatula.

3. Bake, uncovered, for 35 minutes, until the casserole is golden brown and bubbling. Top with the cilantro to serve, and season with salt and pepper.

PER SERVING Calories: 404; Total Carbohydrates: 41g; Sugar: 7g; Total Fat: 15g; Saturated Fat: 11g; Sodium: 298mg; Protein: 26g; Fiber: 2g

Cuban Chicken Stew

ALLERGEN-FREE EGG-FREE GLUTEN-FREE NUT-FREE

SERVES 4

PREP TIME:
15 minutes

COOK TIME:
40 minutes

COOKING TIP:
This dish also works well in a slow cooker. Place all the ingredients in the slow cooker, cover, and cook on low heat for 8 hours.

This sweet and tangy one-pot stew that easily doubles to feed a crowd.

2 tablespoons extra-virgin olive oil

1 onion, halved and thinly sliced

1 green bell pepper, thinly sliced

4 garlic cloves, smashed

1 pound boneless, skinless chicken thighs

Sea salt

Freshly ground black pepper

½ cup dry white wine

1 teaspoon ground cumin

1 teaspoon dried oregano

2 cups diced peeled potatoes

2 tablespoons tomato paste

2 cups chicken broth

Grated zest of 1 lime

Juice of 1 lime

Grated zest of 1 orange

Juice of 1 orange

1 cup frozen peas, thawed

¼ cup raisins

¼ cup halved pitted green olives

2 tablespoons drained capers

2 tablespoons chopped fresh parsley

1. In a large skillet over medium-high heat, heat the oil. Add the onion, bell pepper, and garlic to the skillet and cook for 5 minutes.

2. Pat the chicken thighs dry with paper towels and generously season with salt and pepper.

3. Push the vegetables to the side of the skillet and add the chicken. Cook for 5 minutes, just until beginning to brown.

4. Add the wine and deglaze the pan, scraping up the browned bits from the bottom with a wooden spoon.

5. Stir in the cumin, oregano, potatoes, tomato paste, broth, lime zest and juice, and orange zest and juice. Bring to a simmer, cover the skillet, and cook for 20 minutes, until the potatoes are tender.

6. Uncover the skillet and stir in the peas, raisins, olives, and capers. Cook for 5 minutes.

7. Garnish with parsley and serve.

PER SERVING Calories: 583; Total Carbohydrates: 41g; Sugar: 12g; Total Fat: 31g; Saturated Fat: 8g; Sodium: 1,633mg; Protein: 29g; Fiber: 7g

Turkey Mushroom Stew

EGG-FREE GLUTEN-FREE

SERVES 4

PREP TIME:
10 minutes

COOK TIME:
20 minutes

INGREDIENT
TIP: Cremini
mushrooms,
also called
baby bellas,
can be replaced
with button
mushrooms,
if needed, but
their earthy
flavor is worth
seeking out
at your local
supermarket.

My favorite season for cooking is fall, when the leaves turn golden brown, the days become shorter, and the air has a brisk chill. Here in California, this glorious transition begins in September, although sweater season doesn't come for weeks afterward—but that doesn't stop me from breaking out all of my stew recipes the moment Labor Day passes. This creamy turkey mushroom stew is one of my favorites. Serve with Sweet Potato Corn Cakes (page 75) and a dark beer.

2 tablespoons dairy-free butter (such as Earth Balance Buttery Spread)

2 cups halved cremini mushrooms

1 small shallot, minced

1 teaspoon minced fresh thyme leaves

1 pound boneless, skinless turkey cutlets

Sea salt

Freshly ground black pepper

2 tablespoons all-purpose flour or gluten-free flour blend

1 tablespoon canola oil

2 tablespoons dry sherry

½ cup Cashew Cream (page 23)

1 cup chicken broth

¼ cup minced fresh parsley

1. In a large deep skillet over medium-high heat, melt the butter. Add the mushrooms and cook for 5 minutes, until well browned. Add the shallot and thyme and cook for another minute. Push the vegetables to the side of the skillet.

2. Season the turkey with salt and pepper. Pour the flour into a wide, shallow bowl and turn the turkey in the flour to coat.

3. Add the oil to the skillet. Add the turkey and cook for 5 minutes, just until cooked through.

4. Pour in the sherry to deglaze the skillet and cook for 30 seconds, scraping up the browned bits from the bottom with a wooden spoon.

5. Stir in the cashew cream and broth and bring to a simmer. Cook for 2 to 3 minutes, just until thickened. Top with the parsley and a few grinds of pepper.

PER SERVING Calories: 329; Total Carbohydrates: 7g; Sugar: 1g; Total Fat: 18g; Saturated Fat: 9g; Sodium: 382mg; Protein: 30g; Fiber: 1g

Vegetarian and Vegan

Deep-Dish Veggie Pizza

EGG-FREE **MAKE GLUTEN-FREE** **NUT-FREE** **VEGAN**

SERVES 2 TO 4

PREP TIME:
10 minutes

COOK TIME:
25 minutes,
plus
10 minutes
to rest

COOKING TIP:
For an excellent
gluten-free
pizza dough,
check out
my book *The
Gluten-Free
Cookbook
for Families*,
which includes
a recipe for a
quick-rising
pizza dough
made with
almond flour.

Late one Sunday afternoon, Brad asked for pizza for dinner. I didn't think I had any of the ingredients in the kitchen—just fresh tomatoes from the garden, an assortment of gluten-free flours, and a block of tofu. What followed has to be one of my greatest mom triumphs in the kitchen. I whipped together a gluten-free pizza dough, made an epic pomodoro sauce, and topped it all with fresh tofu ricotta and plenty of fresh basil, olives, onions, and peppers. I thought the pizza alone was enough cause to celebrate, but when Brad said, "This is vegan? It is mind-blowing!" I was thrilled.

1 tablespoon extra-virgin olive oil

1 tablespoon cornmeal

1 pizza dough (suitable for a 12-inch pizza)

1 cup Pomodoro Sauce (page 177) or good-quality store-bought marinara sauce

1 cup Tofu Ricotta (page 29)

½ cup thinly sliced green bell pepper

½ cup thinly sliced red onion

¼ cup roughly chopped pitted Kalamata olives

¼ cup minced fresh basil

2 tablespoons Plant-Based Parmesan (page 27; optional)

1. Preheat the oven to 425°F.

2. Coat the interior of a cast-iron skillet with the oil and sprinkle with the cornmeal.

3. Stretch the pizza dough and place it in the prepared skillet, pressing any excess dough up the sides of the skillet.

4. Par-bake the crust according to the package instructions, about 10 minutes.

5. Spread the sauce over the crust and top with dollops of tofu ricotta. Sprinkle the bell pepper, red onion, and olives over the pizza.

6. Bake for 15 minutes, or until the ricotta is lightly browned. Let the pizza rest for 10 minutes before topping with the basil and Parmesan (if using). Slice and serve.

PER SERVING Calories: 206; Total Carbohydrates: 23g; Sugar: 8g; Total Fat: 10g; Saturated Fat: 3g; Sodium: 520mg; Protein: 8g; Fiber: 3g

Creamy Artichoke and Pesto Pizza

EGG-FREE MAKE GLUTEN-FREE MAKE NUT-FREE VEGAN

SERVES 2 TO 4

PREP TIME:
10 minutes

COOK TIME:
20 minutes,
plus 10 minutes
to rest

**INGREDIENT
TIP:** To make
this dish
gluten-free, use
a gluten-free
pizza dough.

**SUBSTITUTION
TIP:** This pizza
can also be
made with
Tofu Ricotta
(page 29) in
lieu of the pesto
for a nut-free
version.

I really can't decide which I like better—the traditional Deep-Dish Veggie Pizza (page 134) with its classic pomodoro sauce or this flavorful pesto pizza topped with creamy cheese sauce and marinated artichoke hearts. But why choose? They're both awesome.

2 tablespoons extra-virgin olive oil, divided

1 tablespoon cornmeal

1 pizza dough (suitable for a 12-inch pizza)

1 leek, halved, cleaned well, and thinly sliced

Pinch sea salt

1 cup Spinach-Basil Pesto (page 174)

1 cup Cheese Sauce (page 181)

1 (12-ounce) jar marinated artichoke hearts, drained and quartered

2 tablespoons Plant-Based Parmesan (page 27)

¼ cup minced fresh basil

1. Preheat the oven to 425°F.

2. Coat a large pizza pan with 1 tablespoon of the oil and sprinkle with the cornmeal.

3. Stretch the pizza dough and place it in the prepared pan.

4. Par-bake the crust according to the package instructions, about 10 minutes.

5. Meanwhile, in a small skillet over medium heat, heat the remaining 1 tablespoon oil. Add the leek and a pinch of salt and cook for 5 minutes.

6. Remove the par-baked crust from the oven. Spread the pesto over the pizza and top with the cheese sauce. Scatter the artichoke hearts and cooked leek over the pizza.

7. Bake for 10 minutes. Let the pizza rest for 10 minutes before sprinkling with the Parmesan and basil. Slice and serve.

PER SERVING Calories: 728; Total Carbohydrates: 38g; Sugar: 3g; Total Fat: 61g; Saturated Fat: 8g; Sodium: 806mg; Protein: 15g; Fiber: 6g

Mac 'n' Cheese

EGG-FREE GLUTEN-FREE VEGAN

SERVES 4

PREP TIME:
5 minutes

COOK TIME:
15 minutes

COOKING TIP:
If you cannot
find lentil pasta,
whole-wheat
pasta is just
fine, but I like
the added
protein, fiber,
and texture of
the lentil penne.

I tried multiple versions of macaroni and cheese before settling on one that I absolutely love. The simplest option turned out to be the best! The inspiration for this dish came from the book *Vegan Cooking for Carnivores*, which recommends using a dairy-free cheese. It seems like such an obvious solution, but if you've ever tried dairy-free cheeses, you know how finicky they can be! Fortunately, they work beautifully in this saucy noodle dish.

Sea salt

12 ounces red lentil penne pasta

1 tablespoon Better Than Bouillon Vegetable Base

2 tablespoons dairy-free butter (such as Earth Balance Buttery Spread)

8 ounces dairy-free cheese (such as Follow Your Heart Cheddar Gourmet Shreds)

1 cup Plain Nut Milk (page 22), made with almonds

1. Bring a large pot of salted water to a boil. Cook the pasta according to the package instructions. Drain the pasta, reserving 1 cup of the cooking liquid.

2. Return the reserved cooking liquid to the pot and whisk in the vegetable base and butter. Stir in the cheese shreds and nut milk.

3. Return the pasta to the pot and stir for about 2 minutes to combine until thick.

PER SERVING Calories: 548; Total Carbohydrates: 71g; Sugar: 5g; Total Fat: 24g; Saturated Fat: 8g; Sodium: 982mg; Protein: 16g; Fiber: 7g

Lasagna

EGG-FREE MAKE GLUTEN-FREE NUT-FREE VEGAN

SERVES 4

PREP TIME:
10 minutes

COOK TIME:
50 minutes

**SUBSTITUTION
TIP:** I make
a gluten-free
version of this
lasagna with
brown rice
noodles. My
favorite brand
is DeBoles.

This creamy, comforting, one-pan dinner is everything I missed after going dairy-free. It has become an almost weekly staple in our house because it is so easy to throw together ahead of time and tastes so good. Actually, much like dairy lasagna, the results are even better if you make the dish ahead to give the lasagna noodles time to soak up the tomato sauce. Pair it with a side salad and this meal easily feeds a family of four.

**4 cups Pomodoro Sauce
(page 177) or good-quality
store-bought marinara
sauce, divided**

**10 ounces no-boil
lasagna noodles**

1 recipe Tofu Ricotta (page 29)

**½ cup roughly chopped
fresh basil, divided**

**2 tablespoons Plant-Based
Parmesan (page 27)**

1. Preheat the oven to 375°F.

2. Spread 1 cup of the sauce in the bottom of an 8-by-11-inch baking dish.

3. Top with 3 lasagna noodles, then cover with 1 cup of the sauce. Spread half of the tofu ricotta over the lasagna noodles. It will be a fairly thin layer. Sprinkle with ¼ cup of the basil.

4. Repeat the previous step, finishing with a layer of lasagna noodles. Top the noodles with the remaining 1 cup sauce. Sprinkle with the Parmesan. Cover the dish with aluminum foil.

5. Bake for 40 minutes. Remove the foil and bake for 10 minutes more until bubbly.

PER SERVING Calories: 525; Total Carbohydrates: 64g; Sugar: 9g; Total Fat: 22g; Saturated Fat: 3g; Sodium: 995mg; Protein: 22g; Fiber: 3g

Sweet Potato Quesadillas

ALLERGEN-FREE **EGG-FREE** **GLUTEN-FREE** **NUT-FREE** VEGAN

SERVES 4

PREP TIME:
5 minutes

COOK TIME:
10 minutes

SERVING TIP:
The filled tortillas can also be rolled into taquitos. Arrange the Sweet Potato Hummus and black beans on one side of each tortilla and roll into a tight cylinder. Brush the taquitos lightly with canola oil and bake at 375°F for 15 minutes, or until lightly browned. Use the guacamole and sour cream for dipping and omit the lettuce.

I didn't think a quesadilla without cheese was possible until I tried these. The spicy creaminess of the Sweet Potato Hummus is, dare I say, better than cheese. These open-face quesadillas make a quick and easy lunch with their satisfying toppings of black beans, guacamole, and lettuce.

8 (6-inch) corn tortillas

2 cups Sweet Potato Hummus (page 69)

1 (15-ounce) can black beans, drained and rinsed

4 tablespoons cup guacamole

4 tablespoons Dairy-Free Sour Cream (page 173), or store-bought dairy-free sour cream

4 tablespoons cup shredded lettuce

1. Preheat the oven to 375°F.

2. Place the tortillas on a work surface. Spread ¼ cup of the sweet potato hummus onto 4 tortillas. Sprinkle each of the coated tortillas with about 2 tablespoons of the black beans and top each with the remaining tortillas. Place the quesadillas on a sheet pan.

3. Bake for 10 minutes.

4. Top each quesadilla with 1 tablespoon of the guacamole, 1 tablespoon of the sour cream, and 1 tablespoon of the shredded lettuce to serve.

PER SERVING Calories: 488; Total Carbohydrates: 70g; Sugar: 7g; Total Fat: 17g; Saturated Fat: 9g; Sodium: 749mg; Protein: 18g; Fiber: 16g

Chilaquiles Verdes

SERVES 4

PREP TIME:
10 minutes

COOK TIME:
25 minutes

SUBSTITUTION TIP: Tostada shells are available in most grocery stores. Corn chips can also be used for a more deconstructed presentation.

This vegetarian recipe is one of my favorite savory dishes featuring eggs. The tangy salsa verde, crunchy tostada shells, and tender roasted vegetables play off one another to create a powerful punch of flavors and textures.

2 zucchini, diced

2 red bell peppers, diced

1 red onion, halved and thinly sliced

4 tablespoons canola oil, divided

Sea salt

Freshly ground black pepper

4 large eggs

12 tostada shells

1¼ cups Basic Nut Cheese (page 28)

2 cups Salsa Verde (page 176), or store-bought salsa

1. Preheat the oven to 400°F.

2. On a sheet pan, spread out the zucchini, bell peppers, and red onion. Drizzle with 3 tablespoons of the oil and gently toss to coat. Generously season with salt and pepper. Give the pan a shake so the vegetables are in an even layer.

3. Roast for 25 minutes, until caramelized and soft.

4. In a large skillet over medium-high heat, heat the remaining 1 tablespoon oil. Gently crack the eggs into the skillet without breaking the yolks. Fry the eggs until the whites are set and the yolks are still runny, or to your desired doneness.

5. To serve, top one tostada shell with a spoonful of roasted vegetables, a spoonful of nut cheese, and a drizzle of salsa verde. Top with a second tostada shell, vegetables, nut cheese, and salsa verde. Finish by topping with a third tostada shell, a drizzle of salsa, and 1 fried egg. Repeat with the remaining ingredients to prepare the other servings. Serve immediately.

PER SERVING Calories: 739; Total Carbohydrates: 66g; Sugar: 4g; Total Fat: 49g; Saturated Fat: 11g; Sodium: 1,219mg; Protein: 18g; Fiber: 6g

Potato Gnocchi Pomodoro

MAKE GLUTEN-FREE   NUT-FREE   VEGETARIAN

SERVES 4

PREP TIME:
15 minutes

COOK TIME:
20 minutes

COOKING TIP:
Make sure the water for boiling the gnocchi is not boiling vigorously, which will break up the gnocchi.

Gnocchi is often made with ricotta cheese and Parmesan. This version omits the dairy but keeps the lovely texture and flavor of the dumplings. You really don't need any fancy rolling tools for producing the classic gnocchi ridged texture—a fork will do just fine. Or, if you prefer a smooth dumpling, like I do, skip the extra step.

2 pounds russet potatoes, quartered

2 large egg yolks

½ teaspoon sea salt, plus more for the cooking water

½ cup all-purpose flour or gluten-free flour blend, plus more for dusting

2 cups Pomodoro Sauce (page 177) or good-quality store-bought marinara sauce

2 tablespoons thinly sliced fresh basil

1. Put the potatoes in a steamer basket set over simmering water. Steam for 15 minutes, or until fork-tender. Let the potatoes cool briefly, then mash them or press through a potato ricer.

2. Once the potatoes have cooled enough to handle, stir in the egg yolks, salt, and flour. Mix just until blended. Divide the mixture into 8 portions.

3. Lightly dust a work surface with four and roll each dough ball into a long rope, about ¾ inch in diameter. Using a sharp knife or a pasta cutter, cut the rope into 1-inch-long sections.

4. Bring a very large pot of salted water to a gentle boil.

5. In a medium pot over medium heat, bring the sauce to a simmer.

6. Place the gnocchi in the simmering water. Cook until the gnocchi rise to the surface, then set a timer for 2 minutes. Use a spider or small mesh strainer to remove the gnocchi from the water and immediately transfer to the sauce to simmer for 1 minute.

7. Serve garnished with the basil.

PER SERVING Calories: 276; Total Carbohydrates: 53g; Sugar: 6g; Total Fat: 4g; Saturated Fat: 1g; Sodium: 522mg; Protein: 7g; Fiber: 7g

Spinach and Black Bean Enchiladas

EGG-FREE **GLUTEN-FREE** **NUT-FREE** **VEGAN**

SERVES 4

PREP TIME:
15 minutes

COOK TIME:
35 minutes

COOKING TIP:
Corn tortillas
are much
easier to roll
if you heat
them individ-
ually for 10 to
12 seconds in
the microwave.

A similar version of these creamy enchiladas appeared in my first cook-book, *Modern Family Table*, which came out before I went dairy-free. Here they are re-created with dairy-free cream cheese.

1 tablespoon canola oil

1 small yellow onion, diced

4 garlic cloves, minced

1 tablespoon ground cumin

1 teaspoon smoked
paprika

Pinch red pepper flakes

8 cups roughly chopped
fresh spinach

1 (15-ounce) can black beans,
drained and rinsed

1 (8-ounce) container
dairy-free cream cheese

1 (15-ounce) can red
enchilada sauce

12 (6-inch) corn tortillas or
8 (10-inch) flour tortillas

¼ cup minced red onion

¼ cup minced fresh cilantro

1 avocado, peeled, halved,
pitted, and diced

1 lime, cut into wedges

1. Preheat the oven to 375°F.

2. In a large skillet over medium heat, heat the oil. Add the onion and garlic and cook for about 5 minutes, until soft.

3. Stir in the cumin, paprika, and red pepper flakes and cook for 1 minute.

4. Add the spinach and cook just until wilted.

5. Stir in the black beans and cream cheese. Cook for 2 minutes, until the cream cheese melts into the filling. Spread ½ cup of the enchilada sauce over the bottom of an 8-by-10-inch baking dish.

6. Place the tortillas on a work surface and evenly divide the filling among them. Roll each into a cylinder and place in the baking dish seam-side down. Pour the remaining enchilada sauce over the tortillas.

7. Bake for 25 minutes, until the sauce is bubbling.

8. Sprinkle the onion, cilantro, and avocado over the enchiladas before serving with the lime wedges on the side.

PER SERVING Calories: 512; Total Carbohydrates: 58g; Sugar: 4g; Total Fat: 26g; Saturated Fat: 7g; Sodium: 802mg; Protein: 15g; Fiber: 18g

Creamy Polenta Vegetable Bake

EGG-FREE   GLUTEN-FREE   NUT-FREE   VEGAN

SERVES 4

PREP TIME:
15 minutes

COOK TIME:
1 hour

COOKING TIP: Unlike traditional cream cheese, dairy-free cream cheese isn't easily cut with a knife. Think of the cutting step more like scooping it into several small spoon-fuls. The goal here is to keep the individual chunks of cream cheese from disinte-grating into the polenta.

Polenta is usually a labor-intensive dish, but this baked polenta lets the oven do all the work. Even better, the vegetables flavor the polenta from the inside out. Because most polenta recipes call for Parmesan or cream, this version uses dairy-free cream cheese for a nice pop of creamy flavor.

1 tablespoon canola oil, plus more for coating the dish

1 small zucchini, thinly sliced

2 cups mushrooms, halved

2 tomatoes, thinly sliced

1 teaspoon minced fresh thyme leaves

1 teaspoon minced fresh rosemary leaves

8 cups vegetable broth

12 ounces polenta

¼ teaspoon sea salt

1 (8-ounce) container dairy-free cream cheese, cut into pieces (see tip)

1. Preheat the oven to 375°F. Coat the interior of a 3-quart casserole dish with oil.

2. In a large bowl, gently mix the zucchini, mushrooms, tomatoes, thyme, rosemary, and remaining 1 tablespoon of oil. Spread half of the vegetables in the prepared casserole dish.

3. In a large pot, bring the broth to a simmer. Slowly stir in the polenta. Simmer for 5 minutes. Stir in the salt and cream cheese, leaving large pieces of cream cheese intact. Spread the polenta over the vegetables in the baking dish and top with the remaining vegetables. Cover the dish with aluminum foil.

4. Bake for 55 minutes, until mostly set.

PER SERVING Calories: 381; Total Carbohydrates: 27g; Sugar: 7g; Total Fat: 23g; Saturated Fat: 7g; Sodium: 1,884mg; Protein: 18g; Fiber: 7g

Black Bean and Sweet Potato Chili

ALLERGEN-FREE   EGG-FREE   GLUTEN-FREE   NUT-FREE   VEGAN

SERVES 6

PREP TIME:
20 minutes

COOK TIME:
45 minutes

This is a hearty meal made from simple pantry items and fresh vegetables, and it is great for serving a large crowd or for make-ahead meals. It's a versatile recipe the whole family will enjoy.

1 tablespoon olive oil

2 poblano peppers, seeded and finely chopped

1 large onion, chopped

1 red bell pepper, finely chopped

3 tablespoons tomato paste

5 large sweet potatoes, peeled and cut into ½-inch cubes

3 (14.5-ounce) cans fire-roasted diced tomatoes, with juices

3 (15-ounce) cans black beans, drained and rinsed

1½ cups low-sodium vegetable broth

1 tablespoon smoked paprika

1 tablespoon dried oregano

1 tablespoon ground coriander

1 tablespoon ground cumin

¼ cup freshly squeezed lime juice

Sea salt

Freshly ground black pepper

1. In a large stockpot over medium heat, heat the oil. Add the poblanos, onion, and red bell pepper. Cook for 8 to 10 minutes, or until the onion is translucent.

2. Stir in the tomato paste, sweet potatoes, tomatoes with their juices, black beans, broth, paprika, oregano, coriander, cumin, and lime juice. Turn the heat to high and bring the chili to a boil. Reduce the heat to medium-low and cover the pot. Simmer for 20 to 30 minutes, or until the sweet potatoes are tender.

3. Using a potato masher, gently mash the chili to blend the flavors and thicken. Season to taste with salt and pepper.

PER SERVING Calories: 462; Total Carbohydrates: 88g; Sugar: 14g; Total Fat: 4g; Saturated Fat: 1g; Sodium: 333mg; Protein: 23g; Fiber: 28g

Fried Plantain, Black Bean, and Collard Bowls

ALLERGEN-FREE EGG-FREE GLUTEN-FREE NUT-FREE VEGAN

SERVES 4

PREP TIME:
15 minutes

COOK TIME:
15 minutes

INGREDIENT TIP: Make sure to choose plantains that are still a little bit green for a firmer texture.

This hearty and tasty meatless dish takes things in a different direction. Here, I use plantains, which look like bananas but have a firmer texture and are starchier, with only a hint of sweetness. Think of them the same way you would potatoes, sweet potatoes, or any other starch.

1 (15-ounce) can black beans, drained but not rinsed

1 canned chipotle pepper in adobo, minced

1 teaspoon adobo sauce, from the can

3 tablespoons canola oil, divided

2 barely ripe plantains, cut into ½-inch-thick circles

Sea salt

1 bunch collard greens, ribbed, cut into very thin ribbons

Freshly ground black pepper

2 limes, halved

1. In a small saucepan over medium-high heat, combine the black beans, chipotle, and adobo sauce and cook for about 2 minutes, until hot.

2. In a large skillet over medium-high heat, heat 2 tablespoons of the oil until hot. Add the plantains and fry for about 4 minutes per side until deeply browned. Divide the plantains among four serving dishes. Season with salt.

3. Return the skillet to the heat and heat the remaining 1 tablespoon oil. Add the collard greens and sauté for about 2 minutes, until they are just wilted and bright green. Divide the greens among the serving dishes. Season with salt and pepper.

4. Divide the black beans among the serving dishes and season each serving with a generous squeeze of lime juice.

PER SERVING Calories: 337; Total Carbohydrates: 53g; Sugar: 14g; Total Fat: 12g; Saturated Fat: 1g; Sodium: 77mg; Protein: 11g; Fiber: 12g

Crispy Roasted Tofu with Green Beans

EGG-FREE **NUT-FREE** **VEGAN**

SERVES 4

PREP TIME:
10 minutes, plus about 30 minutes to press the tofu

COOK TIME:
20 minutes

INGREDIENT TIP: To press the tofu, halve it horizontally. Place the tofu between two cutting boards and set it on a countertop or over a sink for the water to drain. Set a heavy object on the top cutting board and press for up to 30 minutes.

Sweet hoisin, tangy lime juice, and spicy garlic and red pepper flakes bring everyday tofu and green beans to life. Baking produces a tofu with a crisp exterior and chewy middle—who knew? Serve with steamed white rice.

¼ cup low-sodium soy sauce

2 tablespoons freshly squeezed lime juice

2 tablespoons hoisin sauce

1 (14-ounce) package tofu, pressed and cut into ¾-inch pieces (see tip)

1 tablespoon cornstarch

2 tablespoons canola oil, divided

10 ounces green beans, trimmed

2 teaspoons minced garlic

2 teaspoons minced peeled fresh ginger

Pinch red pepper flakes

1. Preheat the oven to 400°F. Line a sheet pan with parchment paper.

2. In a small, lidded jar, combine the soy sauce, lime juice, and hoisin sauce. Tightly cover the jar with a lid and shake vigorously to blend. Set aside.

3. Place the tofu in a bowl and add the cornstarch. Toss gently to coat the tofu pieces in the starch. Drizzle 1 tablespoon of the oil over the tofu and gently toss again to coat. Spread the tofu on the prepared sheet pan.

4. Bake for 15 to 17 minutes, or until the tofu is golden and crispy.

5. Meanwhile, in a large skillet over medium-high heat, heat the remaining 1 tablespoon oil. Add the green beans and sauté for 5 to 7 minutes, until crisp-tender.

6. Add the garlic, ginger, and red pepper flakes to the skillet. Cook for about 30 seconds until fragrant.

7. Remove the skillet from the heat and add the cooked tofu and soy sauce mixture. Gently toss everything to coat. Serve immediately.

PER SERVING Calories: 191; Total Carbohydrates: 15g; Sugar: 5g; Total Fat: 12g; Saturated Fat: 2g; Sodium: 1,026mg; Protein: 11g; Fiber: 4g

Hurry Curry

EGG-FREE GLUTEN-FREE VEGAN

SERVES 6

PREP TIME:
10 minutes

COOK TIME:
35 minutes

INGREDIENT
TIP: Because
the spices in
this dish are
highly anti-
inflammatory,
this is a great
go-to when
you're feeling
worn down and
want to give
your immune
system a boost.

Aptly named, this curry cooks up quickly. The turmeric in curry powder is powerful at reducing inflammation, and it may play a role in fighting cancer, aiding digestion, and combating Alzheimer's.

1 tablespoon canola oil

1 yellow onion, diced

2 tablespoons grated peeled fresh ginger

2 garlic cloves, minced

3 tablespoons curry powder

1 tablespoon ground cumin

1 tablespoon tomato paste

2 cups chopped butternut squash

1 cup chopped broccoli

1 cup chopped red bell pepper

1 medium eggplant, unpeeled, cut into 1-inch cubes

1 (4-ounce) can coconut cream

⅓ cup vegetable broth

1 (15-ounce) can chickpeas, drained

Sea salt

Freshly ground black pepper

4 cups fresh spinach

½ cup chopped fresh cilantro or Thai basil

1. In a large stockpot over medium-high heat, heat the coconut oil. Add the onion, ginger, and garlic to the pot. Cook for about 3 minutes, until the onion becomes translucent and fragrant.

2. Stir in the curry powder, cumin, and tomato paste.

3. Add the squash, broccoli, bell pepper, and eggplant and stir a few times to coat the vegetables with the spices.

4. Stir in the coconut cream, broth, and chickpeas. Season with salt and pepper.

5. Reduce the heat to low and simmer for 25 to 30 minutes to allow the curry to become thick and rich.

6. Remove the pot from the heat, add the spinach, and cover the pot for a few minutes to let the spinach wilt.

7. Adjust seasoning to taste. Serve in bowls and garnish with the cilantro.

PER SERVING Calories: 368; Total Carbohydrates: 51g; Sugar: 4g; Total Fat: 16g; Saturated Fat: 10g; Sodium: 432mg; Protein: 11g; Fiber: 13g

Roasted Cauliflower Fettucine

EGG-FREE   MAKE ALLERGEN-FREE   MAKE GLUTEN-FREE   MAKE NUT-FREE   VEGAN

SERVES 4

PREP TIME:
15 minutes

COOK TIME:
45 minutes

**SUBSTITUTION
TIP:** Use any
other roasted
vegetable
you prefer in
this recipe. I
enjoy roasted
fennel and
red onion with
orange zest
and basil, too.

VARIATION TIP:
This dish is
also delicious
served with my
White Sauce
(page 179)
instead of oil
and vinegar.

I adore roasted cauliflower as an appetizer on its own or over fettucine for a complete meal. The pine nuts are optional, but their salty nuttiness resembles Parmesan and brings a lot to this Sicilian-style pasta dish.

1 head cauliflower,
  broken into florets

4 garlic cloves, minced

¼ cup minced fresh parsley

1 teaspoon grated lemon zest

4 tablespoons extra-virgin
  olive oil, divided

Sea salt

Freshly ground black pepper

16 ounces fettucine or
  gluten-free pasta

2 tablespoons red wine vinegar

¼ cup roughly chopped
  toasted pine nuts (optional)

1. Preheat the oven to 400°F. Line a sheet pan with parchment paper.

2. In a large bowl, stir together the cauliflower, garlic, parsley, and lemon zest. Drizzle with 2 tablespoons of the oil and generously season with salt and pepper. Spread the cauliflower on the prepared sheet pan.

3. Roast for 40 to 45 minutes, or until the cauliflower is tender and caramelized.

4. Bring a large pot of salted water to a boil. Cook the pasta according to the package directions. Drain and transfer the cooked pasta to a serving dish.

5. Add the cauliflower to the past and gently toss to mix. Drizzle with the remaining 2 tablespoons oil and the vinegar. Toss again to mix. Top with the pine nuts (if using).

PER SERVING Calories: 572; Total Carbohydrates: 81g; Sugar: 5g; Total Fat: 21g; Saturated Fat: 3g; Sodium: 88mg; Protein: 16g; Fiber: 5g

Ginger-Soy Broccoli Pasta with Tempeh

EGG-FREE   **MAKE GLUTEN-FREE**   **NUT-FREE**   **VEGAN**

SERVES 4

PREP TIME:
15 minutes

COOK TIME:
15 minutes

INGREDIENT
TIP: To make
this dish
gluten-free,
use gluten-free
soy sauce and
pasta, and
make sure to
select a brand
of tempeh
that does not
include gluten.

SERVING TIP:
The dish can
also be served
chilled. Simply
refrigerate
in a covered
container until
ready to serve.

Somehow, my kids love broccoli. I don't know how this happened, but when you find something that works, you just have to go with it. This naturally dairy-free pasta is loaded with two whole heads of broccoli that cook in the pasta cooking liquid, so less cleanup and hassle for me. You don't technically have to cook the tempeh, but giving it a quick sear in hot oil yields a crisp, nutty texture that I can't get enough of.

Sea salt

12 ounces spaghetti noodles or gluten-free pasta

2 heads broccoli, broken into florets

2 tablespoons canola oil

1 (8-ounce) package tempeh, cut into thin 2-inch strips

1 tablespoon freshly squeezed lime juice

¼ cup low-sodium soy sauce

1 teaspoon maple syrup

2 teaspoons toasted sesame oil

1 teaspoon minced garlic

2 teaspoons minced peeled fresh ginger

1 scallion, white and green parts, trimmed and very thinly sliced on a bias

1. Bring a large pot of salted water to a boil. Cook the pasta according to the package instructions, but during the last 3 minutes of cooking time, add the broccoli. Drain, then transfer to a serving platter.

2. While the pasta cooks, in a large skillet over medium-high heat, heat the canola oil. Add the tempeh and sear for 2 to 3 minutes per side just until browned.

3. In a small, lidded jar, combine the lime juice, soy sauce, maple syrup, sesame oil, garlic, and ginger. Tightly seal the jar with a lid and shake vigorously to blend. Pour the sauce over the cooked pasta.

4. Add the broccoli to the pasta and toss to mix. Spread the tempeh pieces over the top, and garnish with the scallion. Serve immediately.

PER SERVING Calories: 585; Total Carbohydrates: 85g; Sugar: 8g; Total Fat: 17g; Saturated Fat: 3g; Sodium: 1,010mg; Protein: 28g; Fiber: 8g

CHAPTER ELEVEN

Desserts and Sweet Treats

Avocado Chocolate Pudding Snacks

EGG-FREE **GLUTEN-FREE** **MAKE ALLERGEN-FREE** **MAKE NUT-FREE** **VEGAN**

SERVES 4

PREP TIME:
10 minutes

INGREDIENT TIP: If you have more ripe avocados than you can use, freeze them. Cut them in half, remove the peel and pit, and place them cut-side down on a tray lined with parchment paper. Squeeze lemon juice over each half and freeze until solid. Transfer to a covered container or resealable plastic bag, and keep frozen for up to 3 months.

SERVING TIP: Top with banana slices and chopped toasted hazelnuts.

Avocados make a great stand-in for heavy cream because they're dense and creamy, but their flavor is virtually indistinguishable. The quality of the cocoa powder you use matters, so choose an organic, fair-trade cocoa if you can.

2 avocados, peeled, halved, pitted, and diced

2 bananas, peeled and diced

½ to ¾ cup Plain Nut Milk (page 22), made with almonds, or Rice Milk (page 26)

½ cup unsweetened cocoa powder

½ cup maple syrup

¼ teaspoon sea salt

In a blender, combine the avocados, bananas, ½ cup of nut milk, cocoa powder, maple syrup, and salt. Puree until smooth, stopping to scrape down the sides of the blender a few times to incorporate all of the ingredients, and adding more nut milk as needed. Refrigerate until ready to serve.

PER SERVING Calories: 392; Total Carbohydrates: 55g; Sugar: 31g; Total Fat: 22g; Saturated Fat: 5g; Sodium: 163mg; Protein: 5g; Fiber: 12g

Banana Cashew Mousse

EGG-FREE GLUTEN-FREE VEGAN

SERVES 4

PREP TIME:
5 minutes, plus
30 minutes
to soak

**SERVING
TIP:** For an
extra-special
dessert, toast
¼ cup of
unsweetened
coconut and
sprinkle it over
the mousse
as a garnish.

This creamy mousse is a fun afternoon snack, or you can even make it for breakfast. The toasted coconut milk adds complexity and depth, but if you're crunched for time, use canned "lite" coconut milk instead.

¾ cup raw unsalted cashews, soaked in hot water for at least 30 minutes

2 ripe bananas, sliced, divided

1 cup toasted Coconut Milk (page 25)

¼ cup maple syrup, plus more as needed

2 teaspoons vanilla extract

1 teaspoon ground cinnamon

Pinch sea salt

2 tablespoons coconut oil

1. Drain the cashews, rinse them, and place in a blender. Add half of the bananas, the coconut milk, maple syrup, vanilla, cinnamon, and salt. Puree until very smooth.

2. With the motor still running, pour in the coconut oil and blend until thoroughly integrated. Divide the mousse among four serving cups and top with the remaining banana slices.

PER SERVING Calories: 333; Total Carbohydrates: 35g; Sugar: 19g; Total Fat: 19g; Saturated Fat: 8g; Sodium: 64mg; Protein: 6g; Fiber: 3g

Blackberry Cheesecake Bites

EGG-FREE GLUTEN-FREE VEGAN

SERVES 4

PREP TIME:
5 minutes, plus overnight to soak and 1 hour 30 minutes to set

COOKING TIP: Because you can keep these bites in the freezer, this dessert works great as a make-ahead item, particularly for special occasions. To thaw, place the bites on the countertop for 1 hour to come to room temperature.

That famous cheesecake restaurant doesn't have a thing on this dessert. These satisfying bites are so much healthier with the fat from the coconut, protein from the almonds, and antioxidants from the blackberries. Not to mention the sugar-free sweetness. It's a one-two-three-four power punch. Who says dessert isn't good for you?

1½ cups almonds, soaked in water overnight, drained

1 cup fresh blackberries

⅓ cup coconut oil, melted

¼ cup full-fat coconut cream

⅓ cup monk fruit sweetener

¼ cup freshly squeezed lemon juice

1. Prepare a muffin tin by lining the cups with cupcake liners. Set aside.

2. In a high-powered blender, combine the soaked almonds, blackberries, melted coconut oil, coconut cream, sweetener, and lemon juice. Blend on high speed until the mixture is whipped and fluffy. Divide the mixture equally among the prepared muffin cups.

3. Place the muffin tin in the freezer for 1 hour 30 minutes to allow the cheesecake bites to set.

PER SERVING Calories: 514; Total Carbohydrates: 18g; Sugar: 4g; Total Fat: 48g; Saturated Fat: 22g; Sodium: 4mg; Protein: 12g; Fiber: 9g

Vanilla or Chocolate Ice Cream

GLUTEN-FREE

SERVES 10

PREP TIME:
10 minutes,
plus time to
chill and churn

COOK TIME:
10 minutes

I make this ice cream often enough that I don't even reach for the recipe anymore, which is not such a feat when you see that it only requires a handful of ingredients. I use both coconut milk and almond milk because I want the fat of the coconut milk, but I don't want coconut flavor to overpower the ice cream—half of each seems to be the perfect balance.

2 cups Plain Nut Milk (page 22), made with almonds

1 (15-ounce) can full-fat coconut milk

¾ cup sugar (reduce to ½ cup for chocolate ice cream)

1 tablespoon vanilla extract

6 ounces dairy-free dark chocolate, broken into pieces (for chocolate ice cream)

¼ teaspoon salt (optional; for chocolate ice cream)

2 tablespoons cornstarch or arrowroot

3 large egg yolks

1. In a medium saucepan over medium heat, combine the nut milk, coconut milk, sugar, and vanilla.

2. To make chocolate ice cream: Add the chocolate and salt (if using).

3. Cook for 2 to 3 minutes for vanilla ice cream, or about 5 minutes for chocolate, whisking constantly, until the sugar dissolves and the chocolate melts (if using).

4. In a medium bowl, whisk the cornstarch and egg yolks to blend. In a thin stream, pour ½ cup of the heated milk mixture into the egg yolks, whisking constantly to temper them. Pour the egg yolk mixture into the saucepan and cook gently for 3 to 5 minutes, stirring often, until the mixture begins to thicken. Do not bring to a simmer or the egg yolks will curdle.

5. Remove the saucepan from the heat and pour the mixture through a fine-mesh sieve into a shallow dish. Cover the top surface of the ice cream base with plastic wrap or parchment paper to prevent the liquid from forming a skin. Refrigerate until thoroughly chilled.

6. Pour the chilled base into an ice cream maker and follow the manufacturer's instructions.

7. If you don't have an ice cream maker, pour the mixture into a chilled bowl and freeze for 30 minutes. Stir with a spatula and freeze again for 15 minutes. Stir every 15 minutes until the ice cream is thick and nearly frozen.

VANILLA PER SERVING (½ CUP) Calories: 188; Total Carbohydrates: 20g; Sugar: 17g; Total Fat: 12g; Saturated Fat: 10g; Sodium: 45mg; Protein: 2g; Fiber: 1g

CHOCOLATE PER SERVING (½ CUP) Calories: 265; Total Carbohydrates: 24g; Sugar: 19g; Total Fat: 18g; Saturated Fat: 13g; Sodium: 45mg; Protein: 3g; Fiber: 2g

French Silk Chocolate Pie

EGG-FREE GLUTEN-FREE NUT-FREE

SERVES 12

PREP TIME:
10 minutes

COOK TIME:
10 minutes

INGREDIENT TIP: Read the label of any chocolate you buy to ensure it does not contain dairy.

SERVING TIP: Top with dairy-free whipped cream and dairy-free dark chocolate shavings for an extra lovely presentation.

Silken tofu gives this pie filling a smooth, creamy texture and brewed coffee, vanilla extract, and plenty of dark chocolate bring deep flavor. Compared with dairy-based desserts, this pie is much lower in fat and calories, but still feels like a decadent treat.

1½ cups gluten-free graham cracker crumbs

2 tablespoons brown sugar

8 tablespoons (1 stick) dairy-free butter (such as Earth Balance Buttery Spread), melted

11 ounces dairy-free dark chocolate, at least 60 percent cacao

¼ cup brewed coffee

1 (12-ounce) package silken tofu

1 teaspoon vanilla extract

½ teaspoon sea salt

1. Preheat the oven to 375°F.

2. In a food processor, pulse the graham cracker crumbs, sugar, and melted butter until finely ground. Pour the mixture into a pie plate and use the back of a fork to press it down.

3. Bake for 10 minutes, until barely brown. Set aside to cool completely.

4. In a double boiler or a heavy-bottomed pan, melt the chocolate, making sure no water comes in contact with the chocolate. Set aside.

5. In a blender, combine the coffee, tofu, vanilla, and salt. Pour in the melted chocolate, and puree until smooth. Spread the filling into the cooled piecrust. Refrigerate until ready to serve.

PER SERVING Calories: 308; Total Carbohydrates: 30g; Sugar: 16g; Total Fat: 19g; Saturated Fat: 8g; Sodium: 302mg; Protein: 4g; Fiber: 3g

Miso-Tahini Ice Cream

ALLERGEN-FREE EGG-FREE GLUTEN-FREE NUT-FREE

SERVES 8

PREP TIME:
5 minutes, plus more to churn

SERVING TIP: Top with cacao nibs or a dairy-free chocolate sauce.

This miso-tahini ice cream tastes like caramel and peanut butter, but is free of both dairy and nuts. And it's a cinch to make—no cooking! Miso might sound like an unusual ingredient for ice cream, but it lends a complex flavor and welcome counterpoint to the sweet, creamy maple syrup and coconut milk.

2 (15-ounce) cans full-fat coconut milk

½ cup maple syrup

⅓ cup tahini

1½ tablespoons white miso

1 tablespoon vanilla extract

1. In a blender, combine the coconut milk, maple syrup, tahini, miso, and vanilla. Puree until smooth. Refrigerate until thoroughly chilled.

2. Pour the chilled base into an ice cream maker and follow the manufacturer's instructions.

PER SERVING (½ CUP) Calories: 367; Total Carbohydrates: 22g; Sugar: 16g; Total Fat: 31g; Saturated Fat: 23g; Sodium: 149mg; Protein: 5g; Fiber: 3g

Shortbread with Lemon Curd

MAKE GLUTEN-FREE **MAKE NUT-FREE**

SERVES 9

PREP TIME:
15 minutes

COOK TIME:
25 minutes,
plus
20 minutes
to cool

This flaky, buttery shortbread is perfect with a midmorning cup of coffee.

FOR THE SHORTBREAD

2½ cups all-purpose flour or
gluten-free flour blend

1 cup (2 sticks) dairy-free
butter (such as Earth
Balance Buttery Spread)

½ cup powdered sugar

¼ cup Plain Nut Milk (page 22),
made with almonds, or
plain Rice Milk (page 26)

1 tablespoon vanilla extract

½ teaspoon sea salt

FOR THE LEMON CURD

4 tablespoons (½ stick)
dairy-free butter (such as
Earth Balance Buttery Spread)

⅓ cup lemon juice

1 teaspoon grated lemon zest

¼ cup granulated sugar

2 large eggs

1. **To make the shortbread:** Preheat the oven to 400°F. Line an 8-by-8-inch baking dish with parchment paper.

2. In a large bowl, combine the flour, butter, powdered sugar, nut milk, vanilla, and salt. Mix by hand just until blended. Spread the dough into the prepared baking dish and smooth the top with a spatula.

3. Bake for 15 minutes, or until the top is golden brown. Let cool for 20 minutes before cutting into squares.

4. **To make the lemon curd:** While the shortbread cools, in a small saucepan over medium-low heat, melt the butter.

5. Whisk in the lemon juice, lemon zest, and granulated sugar, then whisk in the eggs. Cook for 8 to 9 minutes, stirring frequently and being careful not to simmer, until thickened.

6. Serve with a generous dollop of lemon curd.

SHORTBREAD PER SERVING (1 SQUARE) Calories: 338; Total Carbohydrates: 34g; Sugar: 7g; Total Fat: 20g; Saturated Fat: 5g; Sodium: 304mg; Protein: 4g; Fiber: 1g

LEMON CURD PER SERVING (¼ CUP) Calories: 184; Total Carbohydrates: 13g; Sugar: 13g; Total Fat: 13g; Saturated Fat: 4g; Sodium: 145mg; Protein: 3g; Fiber: 0g

Chocolate Chip Cookies

MAKE GLUTEN-FREE   NUT-FREE

MAKES
3 DOZEN
SMALL
COOKIES

PREP TIME:
10 minutes

COOK TIME:
10 minutes

INGREDIENT
TIP: I like
to use a
butter-flavored
shortening,
but it is worth
contacting the
manufacturer
to ensure the
product is
completely
dairy-free.

Some chocolate chip cookies call for butter, but the problem with butter (besides the fact that it is a dairy product) is that it melts quickly and contains more water and less fat than vegetable shortening or coconut oil, negatively affecting the texture of the cookie. I prefer baking with coconut oil, or occasionally with vegetable shortening, which works nicely in this recipe.

1 cup vegetable shortening

¾ cup packed brown sugar

¾ cup granulated sugar

2 large eggs

1 tablespoon vanilla extract

1 teaspoon sea salt

1 teaspoon baking soda

2¼ cups all-purpose flour or gluten-free flour blend

2 cups dairy-free dark chocolate chips

1. Preheat the oven to 350°F. Line a sheet pan with parchment paper.

2. In a bowl, use an electric mixer to beat together the shortening, brown sugar, and granulated sugar for about 2 minutes, until light and fluffy.

3. Add the eggs and vanilla and beat until thoroughly emulsified.

4. Add the salt, baking soda, and flour and beat just until blended, using a spatula if necessary, to finish incorporating the flour.

5. Fold in the chocolate chips.

6. Scoop the cookie dough into 1-inch balls and place them on the prepared sheet pan about 2 inches apart. Gently flatten the cookies with your hand.

7. Bake for 10 minutes, or just until golden brown around the edges. The cookies should still be soft in the center. Transfer to a cooling rack.

8. Repeat with the remaining dough.

PER SERVING (1 COOKIE) Calories: 173; Total Carbohydrates: 22g; Sugar: 14g; Total Fat: 10g; Saturated Fat: 4g; Sodium: 91mg; Protein: 2g; Fiber: 0g

Double Dark Chocolate Brownies

MAKE GLUTEN-FREE NUT-FREE

**MAKES
9 BROWNIES**

PREP TIME:
5 minutes

COOK TIME:
22 minutes

**SERVING
TIP:** Top the
brownies with a
generous pinch
of flaky sea salt
as soon as they
come out of the
oven for a nice
contrast of tex-
ture and flavor.

In my kitchen, good-quality dark chocolate is as essential as almond milk
and eggs. But sometimes I want a dessert that lasts a little longer than a
single square of chocolate. Brownies satisfy my cravings, but only when
they're the deepest, darkest chocolate.

1 (11-ounce) bag dairy-free
dark chocolate chips,
preferably 60 percent
cacao or more, divided

½ cup coconut oil

4 large eggs

½ teaspoon sea salt

½ cup packed brown sugar

1 tablespoon vanilla extract

1 cup all-purpose flour or
gluten-free flour blend

1. Preheat the oven to 350°F. Line an 8-by-8-inch baking pan with
   parchment paper.

2. In a double boiler or heavy-bottomed skillet, melt 1 cup of the chocolate chips and the coconut oil. Let cool.

3. In a large bowl, use an electric mixer to beat together the eggs, salt,
   brown sugar, and vanilla for about 1 minute until smooth. Add the
   cooled chocolate mixture and beat just until integrated.

4. Sift in the flour and stir just until integrated. Fold in the remaining
   chocolate chips. Spread the batter into the prepared pan.

5. Bake for 20 to 22 minutes, until crisp around the edges and just set in
   the middle.

PER SERVING (1 BROWNIE) Calories: 347; Total Carbohydrates: 31g; Sugar: 18g;
Total Fat: 22g; Saturated Fat: 16g; Sodium: 135mg; Protein: 5g; Fiber: 3g

Classic White Cake

MAKE GLUTEN-FREE   NUT-FREE

SERVES 12

PREP TIME:
10 minutes

COOK TIME:
20 minutes

INGREDIENT
TIP: For best
results, use
aluminum-free
double-acting
baking powder.

Fluffy, moist, and dairy-free, this classic white cake will become your birthday party staple. Fill it with Lemon Curd (page 160) and top with dairy-free Vanilla Frosting (page 166).

12 tablespoons (1½ sticks) dairy-free butter (such as Earth Balance Buttery Spread), at room temperature, plus more for coating the pan

1 cup sugar

¾ cup plain Soy Milk (page 24)

1 teaspoon vanilla extract

2 cups cake flour or gluten-free flour blend

2 teaspoons baking powder

¼ teaspoon sea salt

4 large egg whites

1. Preheat the oven to 350°F. Line two 8- or 9-inch round cake pans with parchment paper and lightly coat with butter.

2. In a large bowl, use an electric mixer to beat together the butter and sugar for about 2 minutes, until light and fluffy.

3. Add the soy milk and vanilla. Beat for about 30 seconds just until integrated.

4. In a medium bowl, sift together the flour, baking powder, and salt. Set aside.

5. In a small bowl, beat the egg whites for about 2 minutes until voluminous.

6. Add one-third of the flour mixture to the large bowl with the butter and sugar and beat just until combined. Add one-third of the egg whites and beat just until combined. Repeat until all of the flour and egg whites have been incorporated, being careful not to overmix the batter. Evenly divide the batter between the cake pans.

7. Bake for about 20 minutes, or until a cake tester inserted into the center of the cakes comes out clean. Let the cakes cool completely before removing from the pans and frosting, if desired.

PER SERVING Calories: 261; Total Carbohydrates: 36g; Sugar: 18g; Total Fat: 12g; Saturated Fat: 3g; Sodium: 169mg; Protein: 4g; Fiber: 1g

Peach Cobbler

EGG-FREE **MAKE GLUTEN-FREE**

SERVES 9

PREP TIME:
10 minutes

COOK TIME:
45 minutes,
plus
30 minutes
to cool

SERVING TIP:
This cobbler
is delicious
with Vanilla
Ice Cream
(page 156).

Peaches are such a special treat because they're in season for just a short time and quickly fall to the ground. This simple cobbler lets their natural sweetness shine, with just a hint of sugar in the filling and the crusty, delicious, dairy-free biscuit topping.

3 tablespoons dairy-free butter (such as Earth Balance Buttery Spread), divided

8 peaches, cored and sliced

4 tablespoons brown sugar, divided

1 cup all-purpose flour or gluten-free flour blend, plus 2 tablespoons

1½ teaspoons baking powder

¼ teaspoon baking soda

⅔ cup Plain Nut Milk (page 22), made with almonds

1½ teaspoons freshly squeezed lemon juice

1. Preheat the oven to 350°F. Coat the interior of a 2-quart baking dish with 1 tablespoon of the butter.

2. Place the peaches, 2 tablespoons of the brown sugar, and 2 tablespoons of the flour into the prepared baking dish, and gently toss to mix.

3. In a food processor, combine the remaining 2 tablespoons butter, 2 tablespoons brown sugar, 1 cup flour, the baking powder, and the baking soda. Pulse until coarsely ground, but pieces of butter remain.

4. Stir in the nut milk and lemon juice until the mixture just comes together. Place spoonfuls of topping over the peaches.

5. Bake for 45 minutes, or until the peaches are bubbling and the top is golden brown. Let cool for at least 30 minutes before serving.

PER SERVING Calories: 162; Total Carbohydrates: 30g; Sugar: 16g; Total Fat: 5g; Saturated Fat: 1g; Sodium: 88mg; Protein: 3g; Fiber: 3g

Vanilla Frosting

ALLERGEN-FREE EGG-FREE GLUTEN-FREE NUT-FREE

MAKES
1½ CUPS

PREP TIME:
5 minutes

VARIATION TIP:
For chocolate frosting, add ½ cup unsweetened cocoa powder and increase the rice milk by an additional 1 to 2 tablespoons.

Birthdays can be tough on dairy-free kiddos. I remember the first dairy-free birthday cake I made for Brad. At first, I felt intimidated making the frosting, but was pleasantly surprised that dairy-free butter and plant-based milk worked like a charm in my traditional frosting recipe. The important thing is to choose a dairy-free butter substitute you also enjoy slathering on toast. If it doesn't taste good on its own, it's not going to give your frosting a good flavor.

8 tablespoons (1 stick) dairy-free butter (such as Earth Balance Buttery Spread), at room temperature

3 cups powdered sugar

1 teaspoon vanilla extract

Pinch sea salt

4 to 5 teaspoons plain Rice Milk (page 26)

1. In a large bowl, use an electric mixer to beat together the butter, powdered sugar, vanilla, and salt until thoroughly blended.

2. While beating, add the rice milk, 1 teaspoon at a time, until the frosting reaches your desired consistency.

PER SERVING (2 TABLESPOONS) Calories: 186; Total Carbohydrates: 30g; Sugar: 30g; Total Fat: 7g; Saturated Fat: 2g; Sodium: 94mg; Protein: 0g; Fiber: 0g

Coconut Whipped Cream

ALLERGEN-FREE EGG-FREE GLUTEN-FREE NUT-FREE

SERVES 8

PREP TIME:
5 minutes

**INGREDIENT
TIP:** If you
cannot find
coconut cream,
use two cans of
coconut milk.
The remaining
liquid from the
coconut milk or
coconut cream
can be used
for baking or
in smoothies.

This whipped cream is simple, easy, and relatively healthy. You can serve it with Peach Cobbler (page 165), Double Dark Chocolate Brownies (page 162), or whenever you normally serve whipped cream.

1 (14-ounce) can coconut cream   ¼ cup powdered sugar

½ teaspoon vanilla extract

1. Refrigerate the coconut cream and a metal mixing bowl overnight. Do not shake the can at any time before or after refrigerating.

2. Carefully open the coconut cream. Scoop off the top layer of cream (about half the can), and transfer it to the chilled bowl. Reserve the remaining liquid for another use (see tip). Use an electric mixer to beat the cream for 1 minute.

3. Add the vanilla and powdered sugar and beat for 2 minutes, or until thick and fluffy.

PER SERVING (¼ CUP) Calories: 213; Total Carbohydrates: 33g; Sugar: 32g; Total Fat: 9g; Saturated Fat: 9g; Sodium: 20mg; Protein: 1g; Fiber: 0g

Sauces, Condiments, and Dressings

➤ NACHO CHEESE, PAGE 181

Ranch Dressing

GLUTEN-FREE NUT-FREE VEGETARIAN

MAKES 1 CUP

PREP TIME: 10 minutes

INGREDIENT TIP: I like the garlic very finely minced for this recipe, so I use a zester to get a puree of garlic, which disburses evenly throughout the dressing.

Cool, creamy, and just what you crave in ranch, this dressing works great on salads and as a dip for vegetables. Bonus: Unlike store-bought ranch dressings, this ranch is free of preservatives and artificial ingredients.

¾ cup mayonnaise

¼ cup Dairy-Free Sour Cream (page 173) or store-bought dairy-free sour cream

2 tablespoons minced fresh parsley

2 tablespoons minced fresh chives

1 tablespoon minced fresh dill

1 teaspoon minced garlic

¼ teaspoon sea salt

¼ teaspoon freshly ground black pepper

¼ cup plain Soy Milk (page 24)

In a bowl, stir together the mayonnaise, sour cream, parsley, chives, dill, garlic, salt, and pepper until well blended. If creating a dip, stop here. To thin it for salad dressing, slowly drizzle in the soy milk and whisk to blend. Refrigerate, covered, for up to 3 days.

PER SERVING (2 TABLESPOONS) Calories: 107; Total Carbohydrates: 7g; Sugar: 2g; Total Fat: 9g; Saturated Fat: 2g; Sodium: 228mg; Protein: 1g; Fiber: 0g

Green Goddess Dressing

GLUTEN-FREE NUT-FREE VEGETARIAN

MAKES
1 1/2 **CUPS**

PREP TIME:
10 minutes

INGREDIENT TIP: Basil and tarragon are easy to grow in windowsill gardens. I like to grow them, so I'll always have some on hand. Unlike with pack-aged herbs, none goes to waste because I only pick what I need.

Tarragon is an underappreciated herb, but it gets its due in this classic salad dressing created in San Francisco in the 1920s. With a variety of greens lending to the name, this dressing is something special. Try it with Bibb lettuce and croutons.

4 scallions, white and green parts, trimmed and roughly chopped

1/4 cup fresh basil, roughly chopped

2 tablespoons roughly chopped fresh tarragon

2 tablespoons freshly squeezed lemon juice

2 garlic cloves, smashed

1/2 cup mayonnaise

1/2 cup Dairy-Free Sour Cream (page 173) or store-bought dairy-free sour cream

1 teaspoon sea salt

In a blender, combine the scallions, basil, tarragon, lemon juice, garlic, mayonnaise, sour cream, and salt. Puree until smooth. Refrigerate, covered, for up to 3 days.

PER SERVING (2 TABLESPOONS) Calories: 62; Total Carbohydrates: 4g; Sugar: 2g; Total Fat: 5g; Saturated Fat: 2g; Sodium: 237mg; Protein: 1g; Fiber: 0g

Aioli

GLUTEN-FREE NUT-FREE VEGETARIAN

MAKES ½ CUP

PREP TIME:
5 minutes

COOKING TIP:
Consuming
raw egg yolk
increases the
risk of food-
borne illness.

I love this naturally dairy-free sauce. It's creamy and thick, and everything I'm craving on a dairy-free diet. Aioli is delicious as it is, or you can kick up the heat and whisk in 1 teaspoon of adobo sauce and offer as a dip for Sweet Potato Corn Cakes (page 75).

1 large egg yolk

1 teaspoon freshly
squeezed lemon juice

1 small garlic clove, minced

½ cup canola oil

1. In a small bowl, whisk the egg yolk, lemon juice, and garlic to blend.

2. While whisking constantly, slowly drizzle in the oil, a few drops at a time, whisking to emulsify until thick and pale.

3. Refrigerate, covered, for up to 3 days.

PER SERVING (1 TABLESPOON) Calories: 115; Total Carbohydrates: 0g; Sugar: 0g; Total Fat: 13g; Saturated Fat: 2g; Sodium: 1mg; Protein: 0g; Fiber: 0g

Dairy-Free Sour Cream

EGG-FREE GLUTEN-FREE NUT-FREE VEGAN

MAKES
1½ CUPS

PREP TIME:
10 minutes

**INGREDIENT
TIP:** Silken
tofu is usually
located in the
shelf-stable
foods aisles; it
is not typically
refrigerated.

I usually keep silken tofu on hand in my cupboard, which makes this
dairy-free sour cream easy to whip up at a moment's notice. It's useful for
many applications throughout this cookbook and beyond, including in
Corn Chowder (page 58) and Beef Stroganoff (page 114).

1 (12-ounce) package silken tofu

2 tablespoons apple
cider vinegar

1 tablespoon freshly
squeezed lemon juice

½ teaspoon minced garlic

¼ teaspoon sea salt

In a blender, combine the tofu, vinegar, lemon juice, garlic, and salt.
Puree until smooth, stopping to scrape down the sides of the blender as
needed. Refrigerate, covered, for up to 5 days.

PER SERVING (2 TABLESPOONS) Calories: 17; Total Carbohydrates: 1g; Sugar: 0g;
Total Fat: 1g; Saturated Fat: 0g; Sodium: 49mg; Protein: 2g; Fiber: 0g

Spinach-Basil Pesto

EGG-FREE **GLUTEN-FREE** **VEGAN**

MAKES 2 CUPS

PREP TIME:
10 minutes

**SUBSTITUTION
TIP:** Use kale or
arugula in place
of the spinach
for a slightly
different flavor.
Kale is a bit
sweeter and
arugula has a
peppery flavor.
You can also
use walnuts,
cashews, or
pecans in place
of the pine nuts.

Most pesto is made with Parmesan cheese. This version uses a touch of
nutritional yeast and a generous amount of pine nuts and sea salt instead.
You won't even miss the dairy. I love serving it on Creamy Artichoke and
Pesto Pizza (page 135).

½ cup extra-virgin olive oil

3 garlic cloves, smashed

2 cups loosely packed
   fresh spinach

2 cups loosely packed
   fresh basil

½ cup toasted pine nuts,
   roughly chopped

1 tablespoon nutritional yeast

1 teaspoon freshly
   squeezed lemon juice

½ teaspoon sea salt

¼ teaspoon freshly
   ground black pepper

1. In a blender, combine the oil, garlic, spinach, basil, pine nuts, nutritional yeast, lemon juice, salt, and pepper, in the order listed. Pulse a
   few times, then stop the motor, and press down on the spinach and
   basil with a spatula as needed to make sure the blades are reaching it.

2. Blend until thoroughly integrated but still slightly chunky.

3. Refrigerate, covered, for up to 5 days.

PER SERVING (2 TABLESPOONS) Calories: 89; Total Carbohydrates: 1g; Sugar: 0g;
Total Fat: 9g; Saturated Fat: 1g; Sodium: 62mg; Protein: 1g; Fiber: 1g

Salsa Verde

MAKES
2¹/₂ CUPS

PREP TIME:
10 minutes

COOK TIME:
30 minutes

INGREDIENT
TIP: To prepare
the tomatillos,
remove the
rough husks
and rinse
the fruits in
warm water
to remove the
sticky residue.

This tangy salsa verde is naturally dairy-free and makes a delicious accompaniment to roasted meats. It can also be served over Chilaquiles Verdes (page 139) or simply presented with corn tortilla chips for dipping.

2 cups husked, rinsed, and
  quartered tomatillos
  (see Ingredient Tip)

½ red onion, thinly sliced

2 garlic cloves, unpeeled

1 serrano pepper,
  quartered lengthwise

2 tablespoons canola oil

Sea salt

2 tablespoons freshly
  squeezed lime juice

½ cup roughly chopped
  fresh cilantro

1. Preheat the oven to 400°F. Line a sheet pan with parchment paper.

2. Spread the tomatillos, red onion, garlic, and pepper on the prepared sheet pan. Toss with the oil and season with salt.

3. Roast, uncovered, for 30 minutes, or until the tomatillos are tender. Be watchful not to burn the onion.

4. When cool enough to handle, squeeze the garlic pulp from the skins into a blender. Discard the skins. Add the rest of the vegetable mixture and the lime juice and cilantro to the blender. Puree until mostly smooth.

5. Refrigerate, covered, for up to 5 days.

PER SERVING (¼ CUP) Calories: 34; Total Carbohydrates: 2g; Sugar: 0g; Total Fat: 3g; Saturated Fat: 0g; Sodium: 24mg; Protein: 0g; Fiber: 1g

Pomodoro Sauce

ALLERGEN-FREE **EGG-FREE** **GLUTEN-FREE** **NUT-FREE** **VEGAN**

MAKES 4 CUPS

PREP TIME:
5 minutes

COOK TIME:
45 minutes

COOKING TIP: If you don't have an immersion blender, carefully transfer the sauce to a standard blender. Cover the lid with a towel and vent to allow steam to escape, being careful of spattering while blending.

Its simplicity might lead you to believe that this pomodoro sauce is nothing special, but once you taste it, you'll find that its simplicity is what makes it so great. The flavor of the cooked fresh tomatoes is intense without being overpowering. Use this recipe to make the Deep-Dish Veggie Pizza (page 134) and the Potato Gnocchi Pomodoro (page 140).

2 pounds tomatoes, stemmed and quartered

2 tablespoons extra-virgin olive oil

2 teaspoons sea salt

¼ cup minced fresh basil

1. In a large pot, combine the tomatoes, oil, and salt. Cook over medium-low heat for 30 to 45 minutes, until the tomatoes are broken down and fragrant. Remove from the heat and stir in the basil. Use an immersion blender to puree the sauce until smooth.

2. Refrigerate, covered, for up to 5 days.

PER SERVING (½ CUP) Calories: 51; Total Carbohydrates: 4g; Sugar: 1g; Total Fat: 4g; Saturated Fat: 1g; Sodium: 474mg; Protein: 1g; Fiber: 3g

Tzatziki

EGG-FREE GLUTEN-FREE VEGAN

MAKES 3 CUPS

PREP TIME:
10 minutes

INGREDIENT TIP: Read the label on whichever yogurt you choose. Many contain added sugar, which will make the tzatziki too sweet.

Traditional tzatziki is made with yogurt. This version uses plain almond milk yogurt and sour cream for a similar flavor and texture. Try it in Meatball Wraps with Tzatziki (page 107).

1 cup minced cucumber

1 cup dairy-free plain yogurt (preferably almond milk yogurt)

1 cup Dairy-Free Sour Cream (page 173) or store-bought dairy-free sour cream

1 teaspoon minced garlic

1 tablespoon minced fresh mint

2 tablespoons extra-virgin olive oil

¼ teaspoon sea salt

½ teaspoon freshly ground black pepper

In a small bowl, stir together the cucumber, yogurt, sour cream, garlic, and mint. While whisking constantly, slowly drizzle in the oil until combined. Whisk in the salt and pepper. Refrigerate, covered, for up to 5 days.

PER SERVING (¼ CUP) Calories: 97; Total Carbohydrates: 6g; Sugar: 4g; Total Fat: 8g; Saturated Fat: 4g; Sodium: 61mg; Protein: 1g; Fiber: 0g

White Sauce

EGG-FREE   MAKE GLUTEN-FREE   MAKE NUT-FREE   VEGAN

MAKES 2 CUPS

PREP TIME:
10 minutes

COOK TIME:
5 minutes

COOKING TIP:
For an Alfredo sauce, add 1 teaspoon minced garlic and 1 tablespoon nutritional yeast.

Dairy-free butter and flour thicken this simple white sauce. Most white sauce recipes call for white pepper, but it doesn't have a pleasant aroma, so I prefer to keep it plain and season the finished dish with freshly ground black pepper.

3 tablespoons dairy-free butter (such as Earth Balance Buttery Spread)

3 tablespoons all-purpose flour or gluten-free flour blend

2 cups Plain Nut Milk (page 22), made with almonds, or Soy Milk (page 24)

Sea salt

1. In a medium saucepan over medium heat, melt the butter. Whisk in the flour until no lumps remain. Cook for 2 minutes, whisking.

2. Add the almond milk all at once, whisking vigorously. Cook for about 2 minutes, until thickened. Do not boil. Season with salt.

3. Refrigerate, covered, for up to 5 days.

PER SERVING (¼ CUP) Calories: 58; Total Carbohydrates: 3g; Sugar: 0g; Total Fat: 5g; Saturated Fat: 1g; Sodium: 118mg; Protein: 1g; Fiber: 0g

Gravy

MAKES 2 CUPS

PREP TIME:
10 minutes

COOK TIME:
5 minutes

**COOKING
TIP:** Instead
of dairy-free
butter, use pan
drippings or
chicken fat,
also known
as schmaltz.

Good news: Dairy-free butter works just as well as regular butter for making gravy. The important thing is to use the best-quality chicken broth you can. I like to make broth from roasted chicken bones.

3 tablespoons dairy-free butter (such as Earth Balance Buttery Spread)

3 tablespoons all-purpose flour or gluten-free flour blend

2 cups chicken broth

Sea salt

Freshly ground black pepper

1. In a small saucepan over medium heat, melt the butter. Whisk in the flour until no lumps remain. Cook for 2 minutes, whisking, or longer for a more deeply flavored roux.

2. Add the broth all at once, whisking vigorously. Cook for about 2 minutes until thickened. Season with salt and pepper.

3. Refrigerate, covered, for up to 5 days.

PER SERVING (¼ CUP) Calories: 58; Total Carbohydrates: 3g; Sugar: 0g; Total Fat: 5g; Saturated Fat: 1g; Sodium: 268mg; Protein: 2g; Fiber: 0g

Cheese Sauce, Two Ways

EGG-FREE **GLUTEN-FREE** **VEGAN**

MAKES
1¹/₂ CUPS

PREP TIME:
5 minutes,
plus
30 minutes
to soak

This sauce works like a charm in Mac 'n' Cheese (page 136), and on baked potatoes. The flavor is pretty strong, so add the nutritional yeast a bit at a time until it reaches your desired flavor.

FOR BASIC CHEESE SAUCE

1 cup raw unsalted cashews

1 cup Plain Nut Milk (page 22), made with almonds

1 teaspoon garlic powder

1 teaspoon onion powder

½ teaspoon sea salt

1 tablespoon white miso

3 to 5 tablespoons nutritional yeast

FOR NACHO CHEESE

1 cup raw unsalted cashews

1 cup Plain Nut Milk (page 22), made with almonds

2 teaspoons garlic powder

1 teaspoon onion powder

½ teaspoon sea salt

1 teaspoon ground turmeric

1 teaspoon smoked paprika

2 tablespoons nutritional yeast

1. Soak the cashews in hot water for 30 minutes to soften. Drain and rinse.

2. In a blender, combine the cashews, nut milk, garlic powder, onion powder, and salt.

3. **For basic cheese sauce:** Add the miso.

4. **For nacho cheese:** Add the turmeric and paprika.

5. Puree until smooth.

6. Add the nutritional yeast, 1 tablespoon at a time, and puree until integrated, stopping to scrape down the sides of the blender as needed.

7. Refrigerate, covered, for up to 5 days.

BASIC CHEESE SAUCE PER SERVING (¼ CUP) Calories: 196; Total Carbohydrates: 15g; Sugar: 4g; Total Fat: 12g; Saturated Fat: 2g; Sodium: 301mg; Protein: 11g; Fiber: 2g

NACHO CHEESE PER SERVING (¼ CUP) Calories: 161; Total Carbohydrates: 11g; Sugar: 1g; Total Fat: 12g; Saturated Fat: 2g; Sodium: 192mg; Protein: 7g; Fiber: 2g

MEASURMENT CONVERSIONS

VOLUME EQUIVALENTS	U.S. STANDARD	U.S. STANDARD (OUNCES)	METRIC (APPROXIMATE)
LIQUID	2 tablespoons	1 fl. oz.	30 mL
	¼ cup	2 fl. oz.	60 mL
	½ cup	4 fl. oz.	120 mL
	1 cup	8 fl. oz.	240 mL
	1½ cups	12 fl. oz.	355 mL
	2 cups or 1 pint	16 fl. oz.	475 mL
	4 cups or 1 quart	32 fl. oz.	1 L
	1 gallon	128 fl. oz.	4 L
DRY	⅛ teaspoon		0.5 mL
	¼ teaspoon		1 mL
	½ teaspoon		2 mL
	¾ teaspoon		4 mL
	1 teaspoon		5 mL
	1 tablespoon		15 mL
	¼ cup		59 mL
	⅓ cup		79 mL
	½ cup		118 mL
	⅔ cup		156 mL
	¾ cup		177 mL
	1 cup		235 mL
	2 cups or 1 pint		475 mL
	3 cups		700 mL
	4 cups or 1 quart		1 L
	½ gallon		2 L
	1 gallon		4 L

OVEN TEMPERATURES

FAHRENHEIT	CELSIUS (APPROXIMATE)
250°F	120°C
300°F	150°C
325°F	165°C
350°F	180°C
375°F	190°C
400°F	200°C
425°F	220°C
450°F	230°C

WEIGHT EQUIVALENTS

U.S. STANDARD	METRIC (APPROXIMATE)
½ ounce	15 g
1 ounce	30 g
2 ounces	60 g
4 ounces	115 g
8 ounces	225 g
12 ounces	340 g
16 ounces or 1 pound	455 g

SUGGESTED MENUS

New Year's Eve

Cranberry and Cracked Pepper Cheese Ball (page 67)

Vegetable Bake with Cayenne Pepper (page 77)

Chicken in White Wine (page 118)

French Silk Chocolate Pie (page 158)

Easter

Strawberry-Spinach Salad (page 53)

Green Goddess Chicken (page 123)

Shortbread with Lemon Curd (page 160)

Fourth of July

Coconut-Ginger Pork Tenderloin Skewers (page 103) with herb salad

Peach Cobbler (page 165)

Vanilla Ice Cream (page 156)

Thanksgiving

Pan-Seared Chicken with Mushrooms and Cream (page 121)

Bourbon Mashed Sweet Potatoes (page 81)

Blackberry Cheesecake Bites (page 155)

Christmas or Hanukkah

Caesar Salad (page 50)

Steak au Poivre (page 113)

Shortbread Cookies (see Shortbread with Lemon Curd, page 160)

Birthday Parties

Pepperoni, Red Onion, and Cherry Tomato Pizza (page 100)

Classic White Cake (page 164) with Vanilla Frosting (page 166)

RESOURCES

Books

Against All Grain: Delectable Paleo Recipes to Eat Well & Feel Great, by Danielle Walker

Babycakes: Vegan, (Mostly) Gluten-Free, and (Mostly) Sugar-Free Recipes from New York's Most Talked-About Bakery, by Erin McKenna

Cast Iron Paleo: 101 One-Pan Recipes for Quick-and-Delicious Meals plus Hassle-free Cleanup, by Pamela Ellgen

Minimalist Baker's Everyday Cooking: 101 Entirely Plant-Based, Mostly Gluten-Free, Easy, and Delicious Recipes, by Dana Shultz

The Gluten-Free Cookbook for Families: Healthy Recipes in 30 Minutes or Less, by Pamela Ellgen and Alice Bast

The New Milks: 100-Plus Dairy-Free Recipes for Making and Cooking with Soy, Nut, Seed, Grain, and Coconut Milks, by Dina Cheney

This Cheese Is Nuts: Delicious Vegan Cheese at Home, by Julie Piatt

Vegan Cooking for Carnivores: Over 125 Recipes So Tasty You Won't Miss the Meat, by Roberto Martin

Websites

Go Dairy Free: GoDairyFree.org

Minimalist Baker: MinimalistBaker.com

Vegan.com: Vegan.com

REFERENCES

Barnard, Neal. *The Cheese Trap: How Breaking a Surprising Addiction Will Help You Lose Weight, Gain Energy, and Get Healthy*. New York City: Grand Central Life and Style, 2017.

Bottom Line, Inc. "What You Eat (or Don't) Eat Affects Your Sleep." Accessed August 5, 2017. bottomlineinc.com/health/insomnia/what-you-eat-or-dont-eat-affects -how-you-sleep.

De Biase, Simone G., Sabrina F. C. Fernandes, Reinaldo J. Gianini, and João L. G. Duarte. "Vegetarian Diet and Cholesterol and Triglycerides Levels." *Arquivos Brasileiros de Cardiologia* 88, no. 1 (January 2007).

Food Allergy Research and Education. "Milk Allergy." Accessed July 29, 2017. foodallergy .org/allergens/milk-allergy.

Gibbons, Ann. "How Europeans Evolved White Skin." *Science* (April 2015). Accessed July 28, 2017. sciencemag.org/news/2015/04/ how-europeans-evolved-white-skin.

Lifschitz, C., and H. Szajewska. "Cow's Milk Allergy: Evidence-Based Diagnosis and Management for the Practitioner." *European Journal of Pediatrics* 174 (February 2015): 141–150.

Mu, Q., J. Kirby, C. M. Reilly, and X. M. Luo. "Leaky Gut as a Danger Signal for Autoimmune Diseases." *Frontiers in Immunology* 8 (May 2017): 598.

National Institutes of Health, Office of Dietary Supplements. "Calcium: Fact Sheet for Professionals." Accessed August 10, 2017.

———. "Vitamin D: Fact Sheet for Professionals." Accessed August 11, 2017.

Physicians Committee for Responsible Medicine. "USDA Panel Backs Doctors' Complaints against Milk Ads." September 22, 2001. Accessed August 10, 2017. newswise.com/articles/usda-panel-backs-doctors-complaints-against-milk-ads.

Precision Nutrition. "Vitamin D Supplements: Are Yours Helping or Hurting?" Accessed August 11, 2017. precisionnutrition.com/stop-vitamin-d.

Simple Vegan Blog. "Homemade Soy Milk." Accessed August 5, 2017. simpleveganblog
.com/homemade-soy-milk/.

Tai Le, Lap, and Joan Sabaté. "Beyond Meatless, the Health Effects of Vegan Diets: Findings
from the Adventist Cohorts." *Nutrients* 6, no. 6 (June 2014): 2131–47.

The Blender Girl 2.0 Simple Tricks and Tips. "Plant-Based Milks." Accessed August 5, 2017.
healthyblenderrecipes.com/hints_tips/plant_based_milks.

Tokede, O. A., J. M. Gaziano, and L. Djoussé. "Effects of Cocoa Products/Dark Chocolate
on Serum Lipids: A Meta-Analysis." *European Journal of Clinical Nutrition* 65, no. 8
(August 2011): 879–86.

Tonstad, S., K. Stewart, K. Oda, M. Batech, R. P. Herring, and G. E. Fraser. "Vegetarian
Diets and Incidence of Diabetes in the Adventist Health Study-2." *Nutrition, Metabo-
lism, and Cardiovascular Disease* 23, no. 4 (April 2013): 292–9.

Vitamin D Council. "How Do I Get the Vitamin D My Body Needs?" Accessed August 8,
2017. vitamindcouncil.org/about-vitamin-d/how-do-i-get-the-vitamin-d-my
-body-needs/.

WebMD. "Confused about Calcium Supplements?" Accessed August 11, 2017. webmd
.com/osteoporosis/calcium-supplements-tips#1.

———. "Find a Vitamin or Supplement: Vitamin D." Accessed August 11, 2017. webmd
.com/vitamins/ai/ingredientmono-929/vitamin-d.

INDEX

Acknowledgments

Special thanks to the amazing team at Callisto Media, especially Meg Ilasco, Patty Consolazio, and the design team. You are a pleasure to work with and bring out the best in me.

Thank you, Brad and Cole, for putting up with my sometimes-unpalatable attempts at mac 'n' cheese, nachos, pizza, and lasagna as I tried to get the recipes just right. You were tough critics, and the book is better for it. Thanks, guys! Let's make some coconut ice cream, okay?

Thank you, Rich, for your willingness to eat a lot of different things all in the name of recipe testing.

Thank you, Mom, for teaching me early that dairy isn't necessarily the perfect food for people.

Thank you especially to all the vegan and dairy-free chefs who have paved the way toward delicious dairy-free living. To the first person who thought nutritional yeast had a funky, delicious flavor, to the person who discovered that silken tofu makes an awesome chocolate mousse, and to the person who first realized you could milk nuts—I stand on your collective shoulders.

About the Author

PAMELA ELLGEN is the author of more than a dozen books on healthy cooking and fitness. Her work has also been published on *HuffPost*, *Livestrong*, and *Edible*, and in *Darling Magazine* and the *Portland Tribune*. She lives in Santa Barbara, California, with her husband and two sons. When she's not in the kitchen, she enjoys surfing, building sandcastles, and exploring the local farmers' market.

Printed in the USA
CPSIA information can be obtained
at www.ICGtesting.com
LVHW061320171223
766457LV00002B/6